Portrait
of a
Family

The Schoolhouse

ANGELA MARIA BROWN

Order this book online at www.trafford.com
or email orders@trafford.com

Most Trafford titles are also available at major online book retailers.

Printed in the United States of America.

ISBN: 978-1-4269-5896-0 (sc)
ISBN: 978-1-4269-5897-7 (e)

Trafford rev. 03/19/2011

 www.trafford.com

North America & International
toll-free: 1 888 232 4444 (USA & Canada)
phone: 250 383 6864 ♦ fax: 812 355 4082

INTRODUCTION

This is a true story based on the life experiences of these children growing up in the 1900's. It tells of some of the trials and tribulations that they faced during those years. Even though at that particular time they would not admit that they were struggling. Sometimes they actually thought they were well-to-do and had just as much as their rich neighbors that lived only a few miles down the dirt road. The children realized that they had to depend on God as well as each other. This realization kept them going even when their clothes were ragged and the soles of their shoes were worn out. When they were hungry, there was always a potato to eat if nothing else.

Fortunately, the children learned at an early age from their parents and grandparents that religion was a very important subject. Education was instilled in their brains even though their parents and grandparents were not as knowledgeable about the subject as today's families. One thing for certain, was that the families who believed in God did indeed believe. They knew the bible scriptures word for word by memory. The families that acted like they didn't understand the bible did whatever they wanted to do whenever they wanted to and they suffered the consequences.

This is a story that also tells about the love that a family had for one another. Only one person decided that it was time for things to change now that a hundred years had passed. It was time for this one person to destroy everything that this family had accumulated along with the love that they had held on so strongly during the years. This story is about the strength and understanding that was needed for the rest of the family to hold on to what was left of the strong will they always had when their grandparents were alive and well.

CHAPTER 1:

Getting An Education
While Living On The Farm

In 1896 David Strong moved from North Carolina to Tennessee with the hopes of becoming a preacher and farming his own farm. He left his parents, sisters and brothers in North Carolina. He was a very handsome young black man who was mixed with a little bit of Indian and Caucasian. He was still a very young man, around twenty years of age. He worked day and night, not really knowing what was going to happen in the future. Back in those days it was enough just to know what was needed for the basic daily living.

David believed in God's word. He bought a huge bible with large words and read it as often as he could. He learned to read while in North Carolina. When he moved to Tennessee he met a really nice young lady. He fell madly in love with her and they were soon married. Mrs. Fannie Strong was a small framed black lady with a big voice and she was the daughter of a slave in Tennessee. If something was not quite right, she would surely get it straight quick, fast and in a hurry. Everybody called her "Ma" after they got to know her. It wasn't long before there was an addition to the family and soon after that another addition. The family was beginning to grow rapidly and the need for more income was even more important now than before.

David worked for very nice people who were kind enough to recognize that he had a serious need and that he was a very hard worker. The farm owners were getting old and they were not able to do much for themselves let alone take care of a farm. The two Caucasian families that owned the property decided to sell part of the 2,500 acres to the highest bidders. David and his new wife, Fannie talked about it and then decided to purchase the property. After a day of bidding, David finally bided the highest bid and ended up with 455 acres or more of the 2,500 acres. He was expected to pay $3,150 dollars. The sum was expected to be paid in ten promissory notes. Nine of $315.00 each and tenth one would be $314.00 because he had $1.00 in hand at the time of the indenture. Different amounts were paid to cover the interest. The first payment was $189.00, second payment $170.19, third payment $151.20, fourth payment $132.30, fifth payment $113.40, sixth payment $94.30, seventh payment $56.70, ninth payment $37.80 and the tenth payment was $18.90. He didn't know where he was going to come up with this money but he did not want to default, so he professed to work even harder and preach whenever he could.

With all that was written in the indenture the said parties set their hands and affixed their seals on the 31st day of December 1900. It wasn't easy for him to keep his promise. He really worked as if he wanted to have something for his family and their children. There were times when the farming was not enough and he just knew he would have to let the holders of the property have the land back. Somehow, the Lord worked it out for him to keep all of the land for his own children.

They worked and enjoyed a fruitful life with one another; their children grew up and worked the farm. They still had a difficult time even with all of their helpers. They were avid church goers because Pa David was the preacher of their church. For a while he had a little difficulty with the women in the church because of his good looks and intelligence. Ma Fannie suspected that there may have been other women outside of their marriage, but there didn't appear to be any other children as far as she knew, so she continued to love her husband just as the bible said to do.

Pa David became ill not very long after he finished paying for his property. It was not certain what the illness was but it certainly changed his appearance. It made him look very tired and weak. Ma Fannie was in her fifties and not quite as healthy as she had been either.

Her sons were now in charge of taking care of the land while she took care of her husband. Two of the sons had many disagreements about how to handle the crops and livestock. Both of them wanted to be the soul overseers. Somehow they still managed to take care of the business successfully. The third son was not as interested in being the overseer.

As Pa David's health began to diminish there was nothing the doctor could do to help him. As the weather changed from cold to very cold, Pa David's health changed from bad to extremely bad. Soon after the winter, Pa David departed this world and Ma Fannie hoped and prayed that he would go to a better place.

Ma Fannie handled everything very well because she was a strong family lady with family support. Her children immediately stepped in to take care of the responsibilities. Her daughter Hanna was a very intelligent teacher, who wrote the eulogy. Ma Fannie felt that it was time to do something else with the land. She knew even in her fifties that she would need to make some important decisions as to what steps to take next.

On February 23, 1927, Ma Fannie decided to sell two acres to the County since it was for the purpose of building a school for the black children in the area. There were seven men on the County Board of Education at that time and all of them had to sign the indenture as witnesses to the conveying of the acres. Of course, Ma Fannie didn't have a signature but there was an "X" in the middle of her name as her mark. To witness her signature was her son, Johnathan. Once all of the signatures were there on the indenture the school was ready to be built. The school would be named after the Strong family which made Ma Fannie very proud. It proved to be a very good decision because many children received their education from the school and grew to be fine young men and women.

Five years later Ma Fannie decided that she would give each of her children part of the land since she was not able to handle the farming. Each child received an equal part of the property. Ma Fannie left her mark on each indenture on the 22nd day of March 1934. She was happy and content with her decisions. Her children knew that they now had the responsibility of paying taxes and taking care of the business to maintain the property.

The school was finally completed. It wasn't very easy getting to school since most of the children lived miles away and had to walk across many fields and dirt roads. Some of them were very fortunate and were able to ride the new bus to school. Everybody went to the same school with ages that ranged from 5 to 17. Some of the students felt as though they could just graduate themselves from school without going to school back in those days. The children began to voice their opinions.

Old Schoolhouse owned by the Family

Hey! Come on ya'll we are going to be late to school. "Wait up Thomas," said Mary, Paul, Adam, and Ellen. "Run as fast as you can so that the Strong boys won't catch up with us. I think we got them beat today. I don't know about tomorrow though. Mr. Phillips will be very upset if we come in the school late; you know how he is," said Thomas. "I sure would rather go to school than feed the hogs, chase the chickens, pick green beans and cotton, wouldn't you Thomas?" said Mary. "Oh! Ouch! My feet hurt with these ole ragged shoes and socks. I didn't think we would have to do this much walkin, did you? Guess what Adam, I just walked over a kookaburra and my pants are falling down because they are way too big. Give me a belt to hold them up. Please wait on me," complained Ellen. "That wasn't a kookaburra, that was a kookabug," said Adam.

"Hey look, yonder comes the Strong boys! I see Joseph, Dave, Tim, Samuel and John," said Paul. "So what!" moaned the rest of the children as if they were not interested in them in the least bit. Why they were not interested, nobody knows. It was a snotty attitude to take even though the school was named for the Strong family. There was a possibility that the other children could have been jealous of them at that time. Everyone hurried into the two room schoolhouse.

Mr. Phillips was the only teacher at that time. He was very knowledgeable about many subjects and he taught the children everything he knew. Mr. Phillips believed in being as punctual as possible and so did the principal of the school, Mrs. Woodberry. Of course times were very difficult for everyone since money was always very low and ways to travel were very limited. Most of these students should have graduated around 1945 through 1955, but very often this did not happen.

A beautiful fall day was spent inside the little schoolhouse and now it was time to go home and do whatever chores were assigned to each child. Mary had to go home and scrub their only clothes while the boys went out and picked fresh vegetables from the small garden to be used for dinner. Mama Josephine took care of the smaller children in the area as she sat in her one room shack house with the tin roof and wooden porch which was about to fall in and the red dirt roads. Mama Josephine loved to see people coming down that dirt road because she loved company. There was always someone walking around from the field to come just to say hello.

"Mama!" yelled Thomas, "come and get Adam and Paul please, they are bugging me while I am doing my homework and I can't concentrate. I can't stand this place, can't we move to the city?" "Oh!

Thomas, can't you just help us around here, you know your Daddy is no where around when we need him." "Well Mama, where is he?" said Thomas. "I don't have no idear he is probably over to your aunt Erma's or your Aunt Bernice's trying to catch fish or cook some greens or he might even be in Chicago, who in the world knows" said Mama. "Do we have any kind of paper that I can take out to the outer house?" asked one of the children. One of the other children hollered out "Oh! wait a minute, I have to go use it first." Mama jokingly replied, "watch out for the snakes, mice, flies and other creatures out there and don't step in any cow manure cause you know I don't want that stuff on my floor." "Paul, will you go and draw me some water?" "O.K." said Paul. Paul was always so understanding and helpful. "Be careful and don't swing yourself too far over the well," said Mama. "Adam, will you give me that paper it is my turn to use the outer house and I can't hold it no longer," laughed Paul.

It was always a struggle when it came time to use the outer house or wash up, but they lived through it and they were grateful that they had one, even though it was almost the next thing to having to go outside to use it. Even still, through it all the families were very close.

"Adam, didn't I tell you it is your turn to go out and get us a chicken for dinner tomorrow" yelled Mama. "Aw Mama I don't feel like going out and chasing a chicken and ringing its neck and watch it running around bleeding to death." "Can't Thomas do it tomorrow?" "No, it is your turn so you go ahead and get it done and over with," demanded Mama. "Now everybody get ready for dinner and then Its bedtime." "Oh, Ellen," said Mama melodically, "did you milk the cow so we can have some milk to drink in the morning and Mary go outside and feed the chickens and pigs." "Alright Mama," replied the girls.

They finally went to bed and had a restful night except when they heard the dogs barking outside and saw something walking around. They didn't have any windows but strange as it sounds, they did have little holes throughout the walls of the house that allowed them to see small portions of the outside. It wasn't good when it was cold to have the holes in the walls but at the same time, they could use them as windows.

"Get up children it is time to get ready to go to school today." "Aww, Ma, do we have to go to school today?" said the children. "Just get your clothes on I said. I don't matter if they got holes in them as long as they is clean" said Mama. The children yelled, "But the other kids will laugh at us." "They won't laugh, said Mama, cause they got them old clothes too." "What will we eat? We get real hungry during the day" said the children. "Here take some crackers and some cottage cheese and some braunschweiger and sows to school for your lunch" replied Mama. Some of the country folks called braunschweiger another name. They called it goose liver. "O.K. that sounds good Mama" said the children. So, off to school they went while Mama tended to the new baby boy, Aaron, who needed baby food, clean diapers and plenty attention. "Hold on a minute, Adam go wash the baby's diaper out before you go to school." Adam frowned when Mama told him to wash diapers before he went to school. "Hurry up ya'll we got to be on time to school, you know Mr. Phillips will be very upset if he doesn't see us coming across the field pretty soon" said Ellen. "Maybe we should take him some crackers and braunschweigher, and we hope he will like it because it cost a pretty penny," said Mary. "Well, we got to school just in time anyway," said Thomas.

The first thing the children heard when they entered the classroom was, "alright class" as the teacher tapped on the blackboard. "Who is our president? When was he elected?" Of course, the younger sort of looked around the room. Then one of the older children answered the questions because he heard some of the parents talking about it one day out in the field as they picked cotton and potatoes. "I'm telling it on you Pippy, that hurt," said Valerie.

Pippy was the oldest son of Lillie. Lillie was one of the Strong daughters. There were four Strong girls and five Strong boys. There would have been two more Strong boys if they had lived at childbirth. Mama Julia Strong, who was sometimes called granny, could not carry the other two children for the full term. Joseph, Hanna, Lillie, Agnes, and Albertina were all out of school and had started families of their own or gone on to work to help take care of the farm. They were the children of Samuel and Julia Strong.

Samuel, Jr. was around the same age as Mary Grahamwood and still school age. David was older than Samuel, Jr. and he had grown a little tired of school although he was a brilliant student. Certain incidents would really bother him like racial incidents and he would rather be out hunting rabbits than be in some stuffy old two room school house. He also loved to fish and plant vegetables with a passion.

Ring, Ring, Ring went the school bell for lunch. Adam and Paul ran outside with the lunch that their mother had prepared for them. "Wait a minute," said Mary and Ellen simultaneously, we want our lunch too we are starving to death." Um, Yum this is so delicious. What to drink?" said Ellen. "Go pump some water, get the cup and rink some of the water. Hey look the horses have come up from the pasture to the front of the field. Don't ya love it?" said Mary. "yeah, and I love the lunch even better. I'm going up by the school for a private lunch, alright," said Adam. "Well good, go ahead," said Paul.

Mary went and sat down in a quiet spot and along comes David eating his lunch and singing his favorite song, "doodle, doodle do da do da" and as he was walking he made another funny sound. "What!" He let out some gas while I was tryin to eat and it was real loud, that was disgustin!" Mary said to herself.

"Time to come back in from lunch," the teacher yelled. The children had indeed enjoyed their lunch. "Class, it is time for math. Some of you get a math book and share with your neighbor if he or she does not have a book," said Mr. Phillips. "Now the square root of four is what?" Samuel, Jr. raised his hand and answered, "two." "Thank you," said Mr. Phillips. "Now I want all of you to work the exercises on page 10 and turn them in to me to be graded. Once you have completed all of the exercises, you will be dismissed for the day." "Ow! Ow! Somebody hit me in the head with a wadded up piece of paper," said Samuel, Jr. "All right, which one of you did this cruel thing?" asked Mr. Phillips. No one admitted to hitting Samuel, Jr. on the head. The teacher said that if anyone else tries anything like this again, they would get the leather belt. He also told them not to try the sticking a pin in the toe of their shoes either. Needless to say there was no more hitting that particular day. The student's took their long journey home for the evening. It was such a beautiful fall afternoon in the golden fields and the smell of apple and cedar trees.

"Don't bother the bulls, Snoopy. You know they will chase you home and they can hurt you too," said Gracie. Of course, Snoopy did not listen. He went on and did exactly what Gracie told him not to do. As expected, the bull chased him across the field and he was just a hollerin for his mama. Everybody finally got home and did their usual Friday evening chores.

Saturday rolled around and Mama Josephine was invited to a party for grownups only. She dressed up in a beautiful evening dress with shoes and a purse to match. Papa George hitched up the horse and buggy and then drove themselves to the party. Their children stayed home and tried to keep themselves entertained. Once they were out of ideas, they came up with a good one and that was to go to the grown up party. So they all got up and put their shoes on. They didn't comb their hair or put on nice clothes. They went just as they were with a goat walking right beside them. When they arrived at the party Mama Josephine yelled furiously. "What in the world are you kids doing here?" All of them looked up with dusty hair and clothes and said, "Mary told us to come to the party." Mama Josephine said, "ya'll get yo little butts back home right now cause when I get home all of ya'll gon get a whoopin and get that goat home too!"

The children couldn't wait for Sunday to come around so that they could forget about what happened on Saturday. "Come on chuluns let's get ready to go to church. Hurry, Hurry, get cleaned up and put on the clothes that I have washed and starched for you. Shine your shoes and put on your Sunday socks. Get your money for church, it is wrapped in the handkerchief so you won't lose it," said Mama Josephine. "Mama, do we have to walk down that red dirt road or do we get to hitch up the horse and buggy today?" asked Mary. "No, the horse needs a little time to eat because ya'll really didn't have any stopping sense yesterday when you went to town. Later today ya'll can take the horses down to the pond for water. You should have walked yourself to town and then caught the train the rest of the way," said Mama Josephine. That was usually how the Strong boys always went shopping. "But, Ma our shoes will get all dusty again," the boys replied. "Well dust them off again before you go into the church."

Everyone walked to the church brightly dressed with colorful hats and white gloves. Everyone looked so neat, clean and beautiful. The men had on their suits and they looked so gentlemanly and what a sight for sore eyes. Mama Julia Strong loved her brightly colored dresses and straw hats with flowers on top. Mama Josephine was very fashionable and loved her shoes. These two women prayed all of the time, even when they went to the outer house or when they were churning butter or picking cotton and potatoes.

The Pastor of the church began his message with Genesis. "The Lord told Noah to build an ark and to put two of each animal in the ark cause there was goin to be storm a commin, so Noah did just what the Lord told him to do, the peoples didn't believe it though. The storm did come to pass just as the Lord said it would happen."

"But, now Noah had three sons, Shem, Ham and Japheth. Ham was the father of Canaan. Noah, a man of the soil, proceeded to plant a vineyard. When he drank some of its wine, he became drunk and lay uncovered inside his tent. Ham saw his father's nakedness and told his two brothers. The two brothers laid a garment over their father's nakedness. They walked in backwards so they wouldn't see him naked," said the Pastor.

Mary and Ellen noticed something that the Pastor said and they began to question it. They went to their Mother and asked what the Pastor meant by one of the sons laughing at his father Noah and that for some reason this represents the black race. They wanted to know if that was why they were cursed. Of course, this was misconstrued by someone in the church and when it got down to the children they understood that the reason they were black was because Noah's son laughed at him when he drank too much wine and got drunk. Of course, they finally realized after talking to other preachers that that was not the reason why black people were black. "Noah's son was already dark skinned; his father just punished him," said Mama Josephine.

The preacher preached on and on that day. The church ladies left the church saying, "Gul, he show did preach today, didn't he?"

Everybody went home and had a wonderful dinner, and later they went to Mama Fannie's house for dessert because she made delicious cakes from scratch. Monday morning rolled around again and it was quite chilly outside, but there was no way the children were going to get around going to school.

"Wrap up children! It is a little cool outside," said Mama Josephine. "Mama, do we really have to walk all the way across the field to school today?" said one of the children. Mama answered, "how else you gone get there, if you don't walk?" "I can ride the cow over there," said Thomas jokingly. "Don't be silly it is almost time for ya'll to graduate from that school and then go on and get some more education. "Who is that coming up the field with a horse and buggy?" said Mama. "Oh! That's daddy out there with the horse and buggy," shouted the children as they hopped up and down with excitement. "Why ya'll so happy to see him with that old raggedy buggy and he has not done anything else for ya'll. Now all of a sudden he wants to do something like this. Ya'll need to walk to school," said Mama Josephine. "Oh Mama, please don't be upset, he is a very intelligent man, he just had some difficult times with getting jobs and getting around. "Well children, all he had to do was work with Mr. Brandberry. He would have paid him very well if your daddy wasn't so stubborn and had so much pride about the color of his skin. He should have more pride about the color of money that we need so badly for our food and clothes and shelter." "Aw Ma! We don't think it was about the color of his skin because you know they say that that man Mr. Brandberry may be his own daddy and you know what color his skin is," said the children. "Hush, don't you repeat any of that, you know how he gets highly upset when you mention about his mother and father. You know his mother worked for Mr. Brandberry and you know what happened. Well his mother, Mama Tena gave all of her children except for maybe one, Mr. Grahamwood's last name so that is how Daddy got his last name. Are you and Daddy ever going to be able to get along? You all are still married to each other. This is so confusing and I wonder about ya'll sometime," said Mary.

"Hey! Kids, said Daddy, you all get on the buggy, I'm going to give you all a ride to school today." "Lord help me and my children prayed

Mama Josephine, so's that they will get to school safely." Little Aaron was just a hollerin and screamin for his Mama to come and feed him. "O.K. my baby Aaron, here I come to feed you," said Mama. "Whoa horses! Here we are kids you are at school so's give your old daddy a great big hug and I will see you later on. I'm goin to go and see my sisters and Mama Tena down the road a piece," explained Daddy. "Goodbye, Daddy," said the children.

"All right class, today we are going to discuss our lesson in Health. Get your health books out and turn to page 50. Read the first five paragraphs and then tell me what you should do if someone is bitten by a snake. Read the next six paragraphs and tell me what you should do if someone fractures a bone. I asked you to talk with your parents last night to get as much information as you can," said Mr. Phillips.

A chicken ran across the floor and left chicken droppings all over the floor. One of the students got up and chased the chicken out of the classroom. Then a cat appeared on the window sill. "How in the world did that chicken get in here?" said Mr. Phillips. "I know Mr. Phillips, it got under the house and climbed up onto the porch and came through the cracked door," said the outspoken Samuel, Jr.

Samuel, Jr. had become a little more outspoken and very observant. He was normally a very quiet boy. The other children wondered if maybe he had a lot on his mind and sure enough Samuel, Jr. was thinking about a lot of things. Here it was around the year 1945, with World War II going on and Samuel, Jr. getting a little older, the economy was in shambles and nobody knew when or who would be drafted. David and Joseph somehow escaped the war and continued to manage the farm. Also Samuel, Jr. was thinking about the issues at home.

Mama Julia Strong was having a difficult time right about now with her eldest daughter, who was planning to get married and then move to another state up north. It really had an effect on Mama Julia because she could always depend on Hanna to take care of things around the house when she was not feeling well. But, Hanna met a nice young man who wanted to take care of her and he was going to work at a factory that made batteries and many other things plus the money sounded good. Naturally, this excited the couple and there was nothing anyone could say to stop them from leaving the farm. It was the American dream for many black people at that time.

Many relatives left the country life seeking the good fortune in the factories to alleviate the farming hardships and adverse conditions or so they thought. Of course, some people were able to get jobs and some of them were not that fortunate. The factories hired people and later they would lay certain people off from work, leaving them in the cold weather for long periods of time to fend for themselves with a very small unemployment check. The people were happy to receive the unemployment checks because they really helped them get through those hard times. Samuel, Jr. had heard that the lines for unemployment were very long. Samuel, Jr. somehow knew of these things happening and he feared for his big sister and he really wanted this to known.

Mama Julia could not understand why this was happening since everything was so perfect at home; she could not stand for her children to leave her. Even though Mama Julia was a very quiet and calm little lady, she could really become agitated in her younger days and you would know it too by the way she would sling the pots, pans and then pick up her knives in a careless manner. Mama Julia had a lot of Indian blood and the knives were used for everything including hunting. So everybody had to beware when Mama Julia picked up a knife. Finally, someone had to take her to the side and sit her down by the potbellied stove and tell her that you can't keep your children under your wings forever. They told her that in the book of Genesis 2:24, it says, "Therefore shall a man leave his father and his mother and shall cleave unto his wife and they shall be one flesh. And they were both naked, the man and his wife, and were not ashamed."

Sister Agnes said that moving to the north worked for her eldest sister, so she decided that she would try to do the same thing. The only difference was that she got pregnant and the man married her. They stayed on the farm for a while with the rest of the family. One day sister Agnes was out picking blueberries to make a pie for the family and out of the blue appears a snake and it bit her on the leg. Sister Agnes was fortunate to survive that poisonous snake bite. "Mama,

Daddy, Samuel, Jr. come and get me cause I been bit. Call Mr. Tanner down the road, he knows about snake bites," Agnes screamed at the top of her lungs.

Sister Agnes came down with a fever and never really regained complete health. Her husband decided that he would just up and leave and never show up again. Agnes didn't know if she wanted that man to stay or go, all she knew was that she really didn't care. Eventually, Agnes met another man and everybody knew him and his family because they lived nearby. He never married her because she was not divorced from her first husband. The man was kind enough to take care of her and her child while they continued on as if they were married and they had more children afterwards. Sister Agnes went through quite an ordeal. Later, the man that was taking care of her took her away from the farm and went to work in one of the factories just like many other people because it was an American dream. Unfortunately, it wasn't long before Agnes' man had an accident on the job which left him unable to perform his job sufficiently.

Ma Fannie's feathers were all ruffled up about the things that were happening to the family. Ma Fannie was the children's grandmother. She was getting up in the age and arthritis was taking over her body and her eyesight was failing. Everybody knew something was wrong when Ma started to say, "who go dere?" She meant, who is out there? She smoked her pipe even more than before. She still knew when things were changing around her and nobody wanted to upset Ma because she was a very loving person and she took care of many children in her lifetime. When she found out that Sister Lillie was about to get married and run off to some far off place, she hit the ceiling so to speak, because she really adored Lillie. Lillie kept Ma Fannie entertained when her mother and father passed away. Out of pure generosity, Ma Fannie had given each of her own children some land to put to good use. Of course, one of her children became angry at one of her other children because it seemed he had more than everybody else which caused jealousy. There was a big brawl over this, which caused one of her children to lose an eye. The fight reminded the family of Cain and Able in the bible. The difference was that both of these brothers lived to see another day. The family never talked about what happened to the two brothers so it was a hush, hush topic around the neighborhood.

Anyway, Lillie proceeded to leave the farm with her husband, Willie. As it turns out, her marriage went sour and her husband ended up with some of the land that Lillie's father let them use as a wedding gift. She divorced Willie shortly thereafter. All Ma Fannie could say was "Help Me Lord, I will look to the hills from which cometh my help." She really meant just that because as it turns out, the land was filled with little small hills and this made Ma Fannie really feel the Lord's presence.

Lillie continued to search for the right husband and it was a long and trying task for her which led her to marry five times and they all ended either in divorce or death. Out of all of these marriages, Lillie managed to bare three children and their names were Pippy, Leonard and Ralph. All of her sons married and out of these marriages five children were born. Lillie always dreamed of having a daughter of her own but it never happened. She finally realized that this dream was not going to happen so she spent many days with her granddaughter.

There were just a few things that Samuel, Jr. was concerned about even though he continued to study as much as he could. "Why are the children at the other schools learning so much more? I feel as though we are not being taught very much and I think all of the students feel the same way," said Samuel, Jr. "Students, I encourage all of you to go to the library and ask if they will let you read the books," said Mr. Phillips. "Oh, Mr. Phillips, do you really think we will have a problem borrowing books to read?" asked one of the students. "Why do you think this room is not filled with new books and new learning materials? Think about it. We just don't get out and get the materials that we need and we don't read enough. But one good thing about this particular situation, at least the Strong family did try to do something good for the black children in this area. They even bought the land surrounding the school. Anyhow, if you want to learn more than what I am teaching, then by all means go and borrow more books and read as much as you can because it will help you in the long run. I encourage you to go to the library and make sure you return the borrowed materials because they will start to charge you a few pennies for the time that you keep the book. All right, this class is dismissed. Students, don't forget to bring your handmade airplanes and we will take a look at them tomorrow," said Mr. Phillips.

Samuel, Jr. went home that very day and prepared the mule and plow to plow down a field of Johnson and Sage grass. The Johnson grass was very sharp and could have easily cut him. Then he started bailing the hay with the mule and the plow. He could plow all day if his mother would let him. Of course, he was not the only one that could plow all day. It's just that a lot of stuff was weighing on his little mind. The other boys seemed to be able to do all of their chores and come back from the field and have loads of fun. Samuel, Jr. was still a little too young to really understand how problems could weigh heavy on a youngsters little mind. He loved to read and just sort of stay to himself or as close to his Mama Julia as possible. That's why he was the only one out of all the children that she called "baby."

Mama Julia would stand at the door in the evening and holler to the children, "ya'll it's super time so come on in and eat." The boys would knock each other over and run as fast as they could to get in the house. She always told them to get washed up and not to leave the drinking cup in the yard or they would get their ears yanked. Mama Julia loved to bake cakes. She called them her sugar cakes. The neighbors could smell them all the way down the road. Once the chicken was ready to be cooked, she either fried it or boiled it and the chicken was always good to the last little bone. She could really make the collard greens from the garden delicious. The neighbors could smell them way down the road too. Whew, what a smell. That's why the boys would never even think of missing supper time.

Gardening was a mandatory chore for the Strong family children and everybody planted something or other. Without gardening, the suppers would be very skimpy. After supper, Mama Julia decided that she wanted to make another sugar cake for the church meeting. She went to the cupboard and discovered that she did not have enough flour and sugar so she told David to get up and run down to the corner store and get some sugar and flower. She also decided to make an apple pie. David said, "sure thing mama, you know I will go to the store for you." David would do anything he could for his mother even when he was adult and had a family of his own. David's legs were very long and it didn't take him long to get anywhere. As a matter of a fact he loved to walk and run. Zoom! He would be gone and back in a flash.

Later in the evening everyone would settle down and sit on the porch or on a tree stump and just talk about the day as if they were out camping. All of a sudden one of the children would say, "Mama can we stay up late tonight?" Mama would reply with, "ya'll know what time you are supposed to go to bed." Then the children said, "we were just kiddin, mama. Mama would reply with, "Ha! Ha! I knowed you was kiddin, you'd better be kiddin." It was a beautiful night in the country. Sometimes the horses would walk up from the field just to see and hear what was going on. Every now and then a cow would moo. The crickets would sing all night. They would sing so much that they would sing everybody to sleep.

The next day, back to school they all went after a good night's rest. The school bell rang. The teacher called the names to make sure the students were all present and seated. "Alright class did you bring hour handmade airplanes?" The students were very excited about their airplanes and each one thought their plane was the best one. "Yes, Yes, Yes we brought them," answered the students. Mr. Phillips wanted the children to know what was going on outside of the family farm. Mr. Phillips had heard about Mr. Lindbergh's flight to Paris. Mr. Phillips explained to his students that Mr. Lindbergh had an airplane built in six months and he flew straight to Paris. Mr. Phillips said that Mr. Lindbergh was very tired and sleepy but he made it in spite of the problems that he incurred. He was determined to succeed even though he only had water and sandwiches to nourish his body. The plane was featherweight for traveling purposes.

Actually, this was a history lesson as well as an assignment for science class. At that particular time there was still quite a bit of talk about the Lindbergh's. The children couldn't imagine that a place actually flew across the water to Paris. Some of the children wanted to go on a plane ride and some of the children had no desire to get on a plane because they also learned that many people died when trying to reach their destination by plane.

The students learned that Calvin Coolidge was president at that time and many people were without radios and did not know what was really going on so they really needed to go to school to learn what was going on in the world. There were many upset people when they found out what was going on around them.

Mr. Phillips said, "think about it students! Look at all of the events that have happened. The situation With all of those people that were killed over there in Germany." "Mr. Phillips, why did he kill all of those people? I think it was really a terrible thing when all of those people were murdered. Thank God there were some survivors of that terrible event to let give us some insight as to what actually happened," said one of the students. "Well children, some awful things did happen but think about it children, some of us are still suffering and trying to get over the past things that happened to our people when we were forced to come over on the slave ship such as the Amistad and other ships. Of course, we want to get over these things, but it is something that happened and it will always be with us as a part of our history. We just have to channel our minds to learn new things such as math, science, archeology, architecture. Even though Hitler was involved in a very deadly event, did you know that it is reported that he was also an architect?" asked Mr. Phillips.

"Now class, let us get back on the subject and take a look at the Lindbergh family again. Alright everyone put your planes on the counter. Let us look and see whose plane looks more like Mr. Lindbergh's plane. Yes, the Strong boys built a plane that looked like it and they had never actually seen Lindbergh's plane." The Strong boys were natural builders. They were always trying to put things together starting from chicken coops to barn houses.

The Grahamwood boys' planes were built very well, but it looked as if it would have been bigger than Lindbergh's plane. Next, they took them outside to try and see how far they would go. To everyone's surprise, one of the girls' planes flew further than any of the boys' planes. Alright let us go back into the classroom. "Does anybody know why the Lindbergh's went to Europe?" asked Mr. Phillips. From the back of the classroom came a very small voice saying, Oh, I do, O, I do, I do. It was Valerie.

Valerie goes on to say the she had read somewhere that someone kidnapped their baby son right from the Lindbergh's house some time in 1932. The baby was on the second floor so the kidnapper had to climb up the side of the house. The FBI looked and looked for the baby. The remains of the baby were found about ten months later. A carpenter was arrested and executed in 1936. The Lindbergh's could not live with the press and all of the attention they were receiving so finally they left for Europe with their other son.

"Thank you, Valerie. Students you are expected to read as much as you possibly can. I cannot stress enough the importance of reading. By the way, what law was passed by congress to make kidnapping a federal offense if the victim is taken across the state lines or if the mail services are used for ransom demands?" asked Mr. Phillips. None of the students in the classroom knew the answer so Mr. Phillips made an offer. He told the children that if they came to school the next with the correct answer they would receive an "A" for the day. "I also want you to know that Charles Lindbergh also developed cruise control techniques that helped the American Fighter plane for World War. Thank you class for being so tentative," said Mr. Phillips. The bell rang and class was dismissed. "Burr, burr, it sure did get cool today. Do you think we will have a cold winter?" said Pippy. "I don't know said Samuel, Jr. and John, we will check the farmer's Almanac tonight," said Samuel, Jr. "O.K.," said Pippy.

"We still have some green tomatoes in the garden that you can pick, slice and cover with cornmeal, some pepper and some salt. When you finish that, you can put a little lard in the skillet and brown the tomatoes on both sides and they are really gooood," said John. "We got a few onions in the garden too. Mattera fact, man why don't you come over for dinner. Mama would love that. She is gonna cook some taters and some poke chops. Don't that sound good?" said Samuel, Jr.

The children were home from school and there was a lot of ruckus coming from the wooden porch with the tin roof. "Hey! Mama and Dad what is going on and what is all of that noise?" asked Adam. "Well, I tell ya, George came back from over yonder and tells us that he found a body over there in the woods," said Mama Josephine. He told everybody that it looked like the body of a little girl and anyone could tell by the way he looked that he was really shocked when he made it home. "Oh! No, who could it be?" asked the children. "I don't rightly know yet, but we reckon the fellas will find out and come back with the news," said Papa George. Everyone settled down a little bit and then all of a sudden a loud sound came from the house down the road a little bit. It was Mama Julia calling for the boys to come to dinner. "Dinner is getting cold and you still need to eat," yelled Mama Julia. "O.K. Mama we will," said Samuel, Jr. and John.

Everybody gathered around to eat but all of them sat silently with puzzled and bewildered looks. It was going to be awhile before they would stop wondering about what happened to the girl in the woods. This incident even made Samuel, Jr. stop thinking about his family situations for a little while.

Samuel, Jr. and David decided to read the farmer's almanac together. David loved the farmer's almanac because it told him what to plant, when to go fishing and when to harvest crops. He loved farming even though it was one of his everyday chores. Everywhere he lived he would try to plant something. The almanac also told him when to hunt for wild game. He was very good with a rifle and any other kind of a gun. "Samuel, we gone go hunting when it gets cold, O.K.? said David. "Sure man I will go too," said Samuel. "Let's bring Joseph with us, O.K.," said David.

Meanwhile, George had gone home to tell Mama Josephine all about what he saw that night. Mama Josephine was lighting all of the kerosene lanterns when she heard George walk through the door. He told her about the body he found out in the woods. Mama Josephine was very sympathetic towards George that night. She could see that he was very disturbed by the incident and she couldn't stand to see him that way. Mary heard them talking and felt a ray of hope for the both of them. She was happy to hear them talking gently to one another because it made her feel relaxed and she was able to get a good night's rest. She finally went to sleep singing, "I love the Lord, he heard my cry and pitied my every groan."

Thank goodness it was the week-end because wintertime was fast approaching. The rain was cold, cold enough to want to stay in the house especially if the shoes were not warm. Walking to school in the cold weather was the topic for many years. They longed to ride one of the new school buses instead of walking in the cold weather.

Everybody had to work on Saturdays, whether they were working outside or staying inside. "Mama, I need to go to the outer house and use it and it is very cold this morning," said Thomas. "Wall wrap up real good and hope that nothing gets in your way so that you can hurry back," said Mama Josephine. "Mama Josephine, can I boil me some water to take me a bath?" said Ellen. "Why yeah, go ahead and take a bath cause you are a little smelly," said Mama Josephine. "Get some of that lye soap and wash up real good," said Mama Josephine. "Well, I gotta draw some water from the well first," said Ellen.

"Alright Thomas, you, Paul and Adam go outside and chop us up some wood to put in the stove because it is getting awfully cold now. "I think George went hunting with the Strong boys. I hope they will bring us some rabbits back. That sho is some good eatin with that good ol gravy on top of it. I'm goin to fix some mustard/turnip greens too," said Mama Josephine. Mama Josephine and Pa George didn't have very many cows, so they couldn't afford to have steaks and hamburgers in the house. They were barely able to keep enough milk around the house. "Oh! Mama I can't wait," said Mary and Ellen. As Mama was planning dinner, little Johnnie was running around mocking everybody and having a jolly good old time as usual.

Sunday rolled around and it was time to pull out the old winter coats, hats, scarves, gloves and to hope that they were still alright from last winter. What a blessing, when they pulled these things out they didn't have big old holes in them from the moths and other insects. Off they went to church to hear Grandpa Tommy preach the word. Everybody was at his church this Sunday and the church was already nice and warm for them. Dinner was even served afterwards for those that wanted to eat at church.

When the preacher began his message for the day, he told the members to turn to John 7:37 in their bibles. He began to read the "scriptcha" as Grandpa Tommy called it. "In that last day, that gret day of thee feast, Jeesas stood and cried sayin if any man thust let him come unto me and rank, he that believa in me, like thee scriptcha hath said, out of his belly shall flow rivers of livin water. But this spake he of thee spirit which they that believa on him should receive for the Holy Ghost was not yet glorified. Many of thee people thereof, when they heard this sayin, said, of a truth this is thee Prophet. Others said, this is thee Christ. But, some said, shall Christ come out of Galilee? Hath not thee scripcha said, that Christ cometh of thee seed of David and out of thee town of Behthleehem where David was?"

As usual when church was over Ellen and Mary had some questions about what the preacher said even though he was related to them. "Did you hear him say that part about out of your bellies, oooh I hope that whatever is in the belly will come out just like he said it would," said the girls. "I think I will feel a whole lot better won't you Ellen," said Mary. "I sho will," said Ellen. "Gurl we better buy ourselves a bible so we can read about all of this word," said Mary.

The Strong family could still remember when Grandpa David would preach the word at home. A few people would come over to hear Grandpa David preach the word and his words were always words of wisdom because he was always quite wise for his age.

Anyone could tell that Grandpa David loved the story about Moses because he would always mention Moses in his sermons. He loved preaching and teaching about Moses so much that anyone could actually visualize Moses walking around the field with his rod and long beard and when the sun came out in the wintry weather, Moses was like a ray of warmth surrounded by golden wheat fields.

They remembered the time when Grandpa David began his message with Exodus7:11. "When Para shall speak unto you saying, shew a miracle for you. Then thou shalt say unto Aaron, Take thy rod and cast it before Phara, and it shall become a serpent. And Moses and Aaron went in unto Phara and they did so as the Lord had commanded and Aaron cast down his rod before Phara, and before his servants, and it became a serpent. The Phara also called the wise men and the sorceras, now the magicians of Egypt, they also did in like manner with their enchantments for they cast down every man his rod, and they become serpents: but Aaron's rod swallowed up their rods."

"The Lord said unto Moses, Phara's heart is hardened, he refuseth to let the people go. Get thee unto Phara in the morning lo, he goeth out into the water; an thou shalt stand by the river's bank against he come: and the rod which was turned to a serpent shall thou take in thine hand. And thou shalt say unto him, the Lord God of Hebrews hath sent me unto thee, saying 'let my people go,' that they may serve me in the wilderness, and, behold hitherto thou wouldest not her."

Grandpa David always said a prayer after service and everyone would say Amen and go home and carry on with whatever they wanted to do that day. The children loved to run up to Berryhill on Sunday evening. Actually, Berryhill was just a house on a hill but it was where the Strong children lived with their parents Mama Julia and Samuel Strong. There were lots of berry bushes all around it. Strawberries, raspberries, blueberries, blackberries, etc. Everybody visited the Strong's little small house which everybody in that area called Berryhill. Mama Julia made berry pies almost every day. If the children didn't get their pies, they would eat the berries off the bushes.

Not very far from Berryhill was where the Strong boys started a small business. It would have to be a corn liquor business, of course. David made this liquor and let everybody in the area taste it. It was so tasty and everybody loved it. He went from house to house selling it to only people that he knew very well. David never drank the liquor that he made, however he did drink liquor made by other people. They called him a connoisseur. The connoisseur often became tipsy without even realizing it. One night here was a barn dance at the barn and David was as light as a feather. He was moving around about the barn dancing, talking and drinking when all of a sudden he landed flat on his behind. Everybody stopped dead in their tracks and began to roll with laughter. Surprisingly this did not stop the young ladies from asking him to get up and dance with them. The drinking did not seem to bother them because not only were the boys popular and smart, they were as one might say "fine as wine" which were the words that a lot of women used to describe them. This is not to say that some of the other boys in this area were not popular, smart and fine as wine.

Now that everybody was in a happy and party mood, there was still one person, Mary, who didn't seem to think any of the drinking was a bit funny. Mary was different, she didn't laugh at such things. She wanted to remain sensible at all times. "Why aren't you laughing?" said John. "I don't laugh at everything and this seemed a little bit ridiculous to laugh at," replied Mary. "Well get up and let's do the apple jack," said John. The boys were throwing the girls up in the air even with skirts on. Thank goodness the barn was well built with lots of insulation to keep it warm or they would have been pretty chilly that night.

The war was still going on and some of the men were drafted and had to go off to fight for the Americans leaving the women helpless and desirous of the strong arms of a man. The women were left with not many men to choose from, therefore, babies were born illegitimately and the women just took care of the babies without the man because the man usually ended up marrying another woman and having children with their new wives and these children ended up with the father's last name, therefore being the "legal" children. Many men had two sets of children. It got so bad that some of the women named their children with the exact name (first, middle and last). When the great grandparents and grandparents died, they didn't leave wills to them because they had so many children they didn't know who in the world to leave their belongings to. Mama Julia and Mama Josephine had sisters and brothers all over the place. Some of them they knew and some of them they didn't know.

The barn party ended up with a bang. A couple of the guys got into a fist fight. Thank goodness it wasn't a killing fight this time. Naturally, it was over one of the girls at the party because jealousy got in the way. The two guys fighting wanted to date Mary, but of course she didn't think it was a sensible fight even though she kind of snickered under her breath. Everyone walked slowly home that evening, knowing that they needed to get home and go to school the next day. Dave and some of the other boys wanted to go down to the café' to have some more fun. When they finally arrived, they discovered that someone else was running the café'. The manager for that particular day told Dave and his friends to come in through the back door. Dave could not for the life of himself understand why this man treated them that way, especially when the other manager would let them come in through the front door. Dave did not say much about it right then but later on in his life he did talk to his children about that particular incident. He told the story to them in a humorous manner so that his children would not hold the anger inside their minds over something as trivial that, as he did. He knew that they would have other things to be concerned with such as education.

CHAPTER 2:

Farm Life in the Winter Time

The children returned to school and the main topic for the day was the Pilgrims and how they came over on the Mayflower and other ships. The teacher asked the class many questions about this subject and how the Indians felt about the Pilgrims. He also asked how they got along with each other. Some of the children had mixed emotions about these questions because of their own heritages. It seemed that just about all of the black children in the late 40's and early 50's were mixed with something, be it Indian, Caucasian or both.

They naturally had mixed emotions because they loved their parents and respected them mainly because of what they had already gone through since the 1600's and they didn't want to say anything bad about their forefathers. Even though their parents may not have been what you would call "perfect," they still respected them.

Mr. Phillips went on with his lesson for the day. The Pilgrims learned many things from the Indians under the direction of Squanto, after John Carver, the Governor arranged a treaty of peace with the Indians. The Indians helped the Pilgrims catch alewines. This was a fish in the Herring family. They used them as fertilizer in planting corn, pumpkins, and beans. Way back around autumn of 1621. The Pilgrims invited their Indian friends to a three day festival that we call the first New England Thanksgiving. The feast consisted of cornbread, duck, eel, gore, wild leeks, shellfish, venison, watercress, and wine. "Student's, tell me what you think of this menu," said Mr. Phillips.

"What is eel, it really sounds yucky? How in the world do you cook it?" asked Valerie. The teacher told them that it was real simple since most of the food was cooked on an open fire. The bell rang for lunch time.

"I don't know why in the world we have to talk about this stuff. It was way back when blacks were slaves and that is really what we want to discuss. Besides a lot of us is mixed with Indian, Black and White blood. I still think about that and it is hard to concentrate on this Pilgrim stuff. I wonder if he is gonna grade us on this or give us a test or something stupid like that," said Timothy. "I don't think he wants this to be a racial issue Timothy, I think he just wants us to know some of the other things that went on during that time," explained Valerie.

"Oh, alright," replied Timothy.

"Burr, it is getting colder," said Ellen. She was so very thin at that time anyway. Her sister said it was not cold because she was a little thicker than her small sister. "Here, put this hat on your head so you won't catch cold, O.K., now let's sit here and eat our lunch," said Mary. The boys went out and chopped some wood for the school house to help warm it up. They knew they weren't finished for the day.

The bell rang and class began again. Mr. Phillips was not finished with his discussion of the Pilgrims, so he started right in with the subject when the children came back to class and the teacher heard nothing but moans and groans. Plymouth Colony was the second permanent English settlement in America. The Puritans who had separated from the Church of England in search for religious freedom settled there. They came over on the Mayflower and the Speedwell," said Mr. Phillips. As the teacher was talking, two of the students in the back of the room were having their own conversation. This did not sit well with the teacher, so he went back and simply tapped both of them on their hands with the ruler and sent them to the other room. "Now let us resume this subject without any interruptions. Remember students, the Mayflower was bigger and held more people, therefore they were able to reach Cape Cod on November 20. This area was once an Indian Village, but small pox wiped out the Indians in 1617. William Bradford became governor of the Colony. Thanksgiving Day became a legal federal day after 1941, the fourth Thursday of

November, in the United States when World II was about to be over," explained Mr. Phillips.

"We shouldn't have to write about this for a grade. We didn't have anything to do with the Pilgrims and the Indians," said Timothy. Don't be silly, our ancestors were around during that time too," said Samuel, Jr. Even our parents were mixed with some of the Indian and Caucasian blood. Well, look at the Grahamwoods, our grandmother. She was mixed with Indian blood and so were the Strongs plus they were mixed Caucasian blood. "I still don't think we should have to know about them. I ain't gone write a whole lot, maybe a sentence or two," said Timothy. I would rather do some math and measurements for homework tonight. Whew! Lord I'd better go home and pray about this because I already have too much to do," said Paul. It is getting colder and colder especially at night and we hardly have enough Kerosene to keep the house lit up and you know it is kind of frightening." As the children were walking up to the house Mama Josephine was yelling to tell them to hurry up and get their chores done. "O.K. here we come, what's for supper?" asked the children. "cornbread and chicken," answered Mama Josephine. "That's all?" the children complained. "Well, go out there and get a head of cabbage, ya'll know we ain't got much left right now. With this World War II goin on or whatever this highfalutin thing is, we can't hardly get anything we need. The money is already spent," said Mama Josephine. "Well, the Lord will make a way," remarked Adam. Then he remembered that Mr. Phillips for a long while, black families ate what they were given such as chicken, chitterlings, pig feet, pig tails, chicken necks and whatever was left over, because they were still in slavery when the Pilgrims came over. Mr. Phillips also told the class that later on when Black Americans were emancipated; they learned from their grandmothers how to prepare other foods. Not the scraps that were thrown out to them. They learned about large turkeys, big pans of cornbread dressing, giblet gravy, big rolls, peas, corn, tea with lemons, and greens, well seasoned with a good sized piece of salt pork. He told the class that Black Americans learned to make sweet potato pies and coconut cakes topped with pineapples and cherries. They learned to cook all kinds of stuff and everybody got big and fat except for the people who kept busy and didn't sit down all of the time in a rocking chair. Then he laughed as if he was joking.

In class the very next day, Mr. Phillips said, "I have a few questions for each of you to answer and I want you to write an essay. Your answers will be graded and recorded as part of your language arts grade. The first question is, what are you thankful for? The second question is, why do you think we are discussing Thanksgiving? The third question is, who are you thankful for? Alright class dismissed," said Mr. Phillips.

"Why do we have to talk about this subject? It didn't have anything to do with us," said Timothy. I am goin to make my essay very short and sweet." "Well, look at it this way, it doesn't hurt to know as much as you possibly can," said Mr. Phillips. "Well then Timothy, exactly what are you thankful for?" said Samuel. Timothy replied with, "I am thankful for my mother. I can always go to her for any problem I have and she always has a good answer." "Now, what was so hard about that," said Samuel. "This is going to be an easy subject. Let's go home and get some dinner and later we can go fishing, O.K.," said Timothy.

The next day when the children went to school, the teacher said "Alright class, settle down. We will start the day with the assignment that I gave you yesterday. A very simple assignment I might add. Does everyone have their essays today? I want to start from the left side of the room with each student reading his/her essay aloud. Pippy, I want you to read yours first," said the teacher. "Yes, Mr. Phillips, said Pippy. I am thankful for my mama and daddy for all they do for me and my brothers. I am thankful for the food and clothes that they provide for us. I am thankful for the house that we live in. I am thankful for the livestock that God gave us. I am thankful for my granny and granddad. I am thankful that I am alive today and I am thankful for the school that I go to. I am thankful for God's grace and mercy." "Thank you for reading your essay to us Pippy. You may be seated," said the teacher. Of course, the students enjoyed that essay and began to clap their hands. "Alright, Valerie, please read your essay," said Mr. Phillips. "Yes Sir, Mr. Phillips, I am thankful to God for supplying all of my needs even though it gets hard sometime down here, I am still thankful for him. Then I am thankful for my grandma, granddad, my mama, my daddy, my sisters and brothers. I am thankful for the food, shelter, and clothes that I have in my closet." "Good for you, Valerie. Alright next student, Tim," said Mr. Phillips. "Me, you want me to read my essay now?" asked Tim. "O.K., Mr. Phillips, I am really thankful for my mother because she listens to all of my problems and she helps me with any question that I have about anything. I am thankful for my grandmother because she helped my mother when she couldn't take care of us. I am thankful for my granddad for taking care of us too. I am thankful for my brother for helping when I need him and I am thankful to God," said Tim. "Thank you Tim, that was very good. Alright class, it is time for lunch. Everyone line up to use the outer house and wash your hands before you eat!" shouted Mr. Phillips.

When class resumed, the rest of the children read their essays. They were all very cooperative with this assignment and realized that in spite of everything they still had something to be thankful for. Each student went home that day with very light hearts as if they had really made their contributions to society.

Mama Julia was working on some quilts to give to family members as Christmas gifts and Christmas was fast approaching. The quilts were very beautiful. Each piece of cloth was specially picked for each person that was going to get a quilt. She would give each of her daughters an exclusive quilt especially now that they were all married and had children that needed bedding. They would come in handy since the winters in the north seemed long and bitterly cold. Joseph had also recently gotten married. His bride's name was Jena. Mama Julia loved making quilts in her spare time or even while she was cooking, washing, or at church. Samuel, Sr. worked on his parent's farm, and he usually had some extra money to buy trousers and brogans for his boys and maybe a dress or something for his girls even though they were married and gone. All of this buying had to be done whenever the time permitted because traveling to the city was hardly ever thought of, especially for just shopping.

Mama Josephine was busy in her kitchen making preserves. She loved apple and peach preserves and she would give them as her special gifts.

Everybody loved her gifts too. Sometimes she would take them to different families and sell them. She also took some of her gifts to the church. Some of the members insisted upon purchasing them. This was O.K. with Mama Josephine. Daddy George usually saved a little bit of his earnings for his children, which really was all he could spare. He did a lot of farming for Mr. Branberry and much of his earnings came from helping Mr. Branberry. Mr. Branberry taught him very well about farming and Daddy George used this knowledge to help other farmers around the area.

Finally it was time for turkey and dressing. Thanksgiving was the time when families joined together in the preparation of the feast. Mama Julia, her daughters and sons prepared the hens and chickens along with the dressing. The gravy was made by Daddy Samuel, who was a professional gravy maker. They had cornbread, good ole biscuits, mustard greens, snapped green beans, candied sweet potatoes, cranberries, coconut cake and sweet potato pie. David made some red wine long before Thanksgiving and Joseph made some tea to drink. It was so delicious and you best to believe, it was all eaten up and nothing was leftover. There was no way anyone could go back to the pots and pans and think they were going to get something else to eat. After dinner everyone sat down and talked about any and everything. Samuel would have to begin the conversation with something like, "you know old Roosevelt went down to the barn and stepped on a snake. That old rascal is always getting into something and Lula Bee keeps on hanging them old raggedy draws on the line soz everybody can see them old thangs. I tell you, I wish some of these people would get some sense. I thank they all just plain ain't got no sense atall. They musta be some fools or something." Mama Julia said to Papa Samuel, "you oughta stop talking about folks, they ain't done nothing to you." "Why can't I talk bout em if I want to, they my relatives ain't they?" asked Papa Samuel. "I don't care if they are yo relatives, they still have feelins too. Look at ya, you ain't perfect. You won't even let the kids pick a apple off the tree," said Mama Julia. "Aw, they don't need to be pickin my apples off my tree," said Papa Samuel. "Why not, they gone rot and da birds gone eat em up? Gwoin boy sit down and read the bible. Oh! John, go out and get the mail out of the mailbox. Samuel, Jr., baby, would you go out with him?" said Mama Julia. "O.K. mama we haven't checked the mail in quite some time," said John. It was a little slippery out since it had rained and frozen a little bit. To their surprise, a letter from Hanna, a letter from Albertina and a tax bill for the farm had arrived. As a prank, John and Samuel got it in their heads to go and look in the Grahamwood's mailbox. As they were snooping, they found a letter to Mary from a friend of hers named Charles. The two boys opened the letter and read it together not to mention taking it home with them. They thought they had really done something by stealing Mary's mail. They went as far as to show the letter to David. The word got back around the Mary, and when she heard about it, needless to say she was furious. First of all she was furious because they invaded the privacy of the Grahamwood's mailbox and secondly for showing it to David. She wanted the letter back regardless of the condition. The boys realized the wrong that they had done and sheepishly returned the letter back to her.

Charlie came over to visit with Mary on Thanksgiving Day. It was not uncommon for people to just stop by their neighbors' house uninvited for conversation or even have dinner. He eventually got around to asking her if she received the letter. Of course, she could be truthful and tell him that two of the Strong boys got the letter out of the mailbox but she didn't quite know how Charles would react to the news. There would be only way to find out and that would be to tell him but she simply couldn't tell him. Mary said, "Oh! That letter never showed up, it must have ended up in someone else's mailbox. Oh well, there is a first time for everything." Charles was a bit puzzled about the way Mary was acting. "That is very true, Mary," said Charles. Mary sighed with relief after that subject was over. Mama Josephine appeared in the living area and said "better have some dinner." Charles turned down the offer because he had already eaten.

As they were sitting there talking, a loud noise came from outside. It was the Strong boys hunting for rabbits in the same area that the Grahmwood's lived. Everybody looked out to see what was going on. Papa George looked out and said "what are you Strong boys doing out there?" "We're going hunting, Mr. Grahamwood, do you want to join us?" replied the boys. "I sho do, wait a minute I'll be right out." Everybody in the room turned around and looked at each other with their mouths wide open as if to say what is wrong with him. First he was fussing at them and then he went out and joined them. "Hey man, did ya'll see that little bit of snow?" said Papa George. "Looks like it is going to be colder than we thought. This means we better get things ready for the winter. We better prepare some of the livestock," said Joseph.

After the hunting trip, Daddy Samuel called the boys together to let them know what they needed to do. Daddy Samuel wanted them to get the pigs ready. David really didn't like this job but Daddy Samuel chose him to do it because he knew that David was stronger than the other boys. David had a soft spot for the animals especially the ones that he raised. David loved to watch them grow up and get big and fat. It just simply fascinated him. Sooner or later he would come to the realization that they had to eat and it was either the pigs or starve from hunger. He had to first of all, hit the hog in the head with a sledgehammer and then the hog would start squeeling very loud. It was just plain gruesome. The blood gushed out all over everywhere. Once the pig was near dead, David and his brothers would lift the pig into a barrel of boiling water over a fire to get as much of the impurities out as they could. It also helped with the removal of pig hairs and skin. Then the process became more gruesome. If they had weak stomachs, they could not stand to look at the pig. The slit the pig open and they would take all of the insides out. Then they "slat" the pig. This was when they cut the hog up in different parts so they would have meat for the winter. This procedure didn't bother the Strong boys because they were so used to doing this. They didn't even think about not eating it when it was ready to be cooked. It was some of the best eatin especially after it was cooked in the barbeque pit.

It was clear that Christmas was near because the people were out in the woods looking for a tree to put in their homes. They usually found one in the field and chopped it down and took it home to decorate. The kids loved to decorate the trees with strands of popcorn. Their parents didn't care too much for the decorating but they did all they could to get gifts for their children to make Christmas as enjoyable as possible. Mama Josephine insisted that her children go to church the whole month of December. They went to hear Grandad Reverand

Thomas preach about the birth of Jesus Christ. They know this portion of the bible inside and out because they were out of school for the season. Ellen asked Mary how it was possible that Mary conceived a child without being with a man. Mary had the responsibility of trying to explain how that happened. Mary explained that first of all it was Immaculate Conception. "Well what is that?" questioned all of Mary's siblings. "It means that God chose Mary to conceive the baby Jesus," said Mary. "Well, howz come all the Marys now-a-days have to be married first to get a baby?" asked the siblings. "Oh, ya'll ask too many questions and some of them are just plain silly, so go and ask the preacher cause I'm sure he knows the answers. I have to do something more important like go and milk the cow." "Remember to bend your thumb so you or the cow won't get no germs," laughed Thomas. Ellen began to pout, "I just wanted to know how Mary could conceive without a man, that's all."

"Mama Josephine, we ain't got no oatmeal," said Mary. "I know we don't, I want you to go up to Mama Julia's and see if maybe they got some," said Mama Josephine. Mary tried her very best to get Thomas to go and get the oatmeal but he told her that she know she wanted to go up there anyway so she could see what was going on. Mary was naturally like that, she always wanted to know what was going on with people and their business. Thomas knew that she also wanted to see David. They already knew that she wanted to go up there. She finally gave in and went on up to Mama Julia's house.

There was a rumor going around that Mary wanted to go to another school next year. Everybody around town had heard that she wanted to go to the school for girls. It was something like a boarding school. They wondered why she wanted to go to that kind of a school and leave her sisters and brothers with all of the chores. They wondered what was wrong with going to Mt. Olive school just down the road a bit. Then they were informed that that school grade levels went up to the twelfth and she really was trying to graduate. Adam and Paul thought that she wanted to leave because she was tired of how they were living around there.

Mary came back from Mama Julia's house with a bag full of oatmeal. "She sure is nice, ain't she?" said Thomas. "Yes, and so is David," said Mary. "You are going to get into trouble looking at that boy," said Thomas. "Mama Josephine, can I boil me some water and take a bath?" said Paul. "Go ahead, but make sure it is really warm because it is cold in here and you know you ketch colds easy. Then I have to give you some cod liver oil."

School resumed for a few more weeks and the students were out for winter break. The students were having a ball, well some of them were. Most of them went on with their daily chores and the Grahamwood children were still sad about the rumor that Mary intended to leave to go to another school. Christmas Eve was just a few days away. Everyone was decorating their homes for Christmas. It was now time to prepare another fabulous dinner. This time they would have ham with a glaze over it and of course there would be a hen with dressing, collard greens, cornbread, potatoes, butter beans, pudding cake and tea to drink. Mary and Ellen usually made some oatmeal cookies with raisins in them. On Christmas Eve all of their presents were placed under the tree. Mary got a new pair of shoes, Ellen got a new dress, Thomas got a new suit of clothes, Adam got a new shirt, Paul got a new pair of pants, and little Aaron got a new toy truck to play with. The children were all pleased with their gifts and thanked their mama and daddy with hugs and kisses. The children saved some money and they put it all together and gave it to Mama Josephine and Daddy George.

Since all of the people in this area were like one big happy family, of course the Grahamwood children got up and went over to the Strong's house to see what they got for Christmas. David, Samuel, John and Tim were the only children still living at home but Christmas was still a very happy time. They got their Mama Julia a new cooking pot and they got Daddy Samuel a new three piece suit. Everybody was happy with their gifts.

Later that day, Charles came by to visit Mary again. He gave her a gift that she really liked. It was a beautiful necklace. Valerie came by and asked Mary if she wanted to go out on a date with her and her date. They did get to go to a dance and had a wonderful holiday party. Everybody happened to be there just as they were at the barn party. No drinking was aloud this time but there was a lot of hugging and kissing which was also a no, no as far as their parents were concerned. Since it was cold outside the teenagers found it quite easy to snuggle up with each other and none of them gave their parents a second thought at that time.

After the holiday party, Mama Josephine met the girls at the house. What a surprise for the girls, who were cousins and on top of that they were very close but they got into a lot of trouble when they were together. Mama Josephine chastised the girls for staying out so late with the boys. There was no telling what could have happened to the two girls. "Listen here young ladies, I don't want you to come in the house this late at night ever again! You hear me talking to ya?" Mama Josephine. "Yes Mam," said the two girls. "So now let us pray about this right now and pray that these boys won't bother ya later on. Don't talk back to me either cause I just told ya what I want ya to do. Now I am gonna say it again and I don't want you two to say another word or ya'll gonna get the whipping of your lives right in front of these boys. Now Valerie let Adam and Paul walk you home and that's the end of it ya hear?" said Mama Josephine. "Yes Mam, see you tomorrow Mary, the Lord willing and the creek don't rise," said Valerie.

As the boys were walking Valerie home, they were wondering what in the world got into their mother and why did she fuss at them so much because she never did that before. The only thing they could come up with was that she was really not feeling good or Daddy George had done something she didn't like. Anyway it was all over now they were thankful for that.

The Christmas break was just about over and pretty soon it would be time to go back to school and of course the student were not happy because it meant homework and making nightly preparations to get up and go to school. In a way, they were kind of lucky that there was still snow and ice from the night before and more snow came while they were asleep, but in a way they were not lucky because it was very cold in the thinly insulated homes where they lived. They had to keep putting wood in the pot bellied stoves they had to keep the rooms warm, not to mention getting up and going outside to use the outer house. Thank goodness for the gift from Mama Julia to cover them up. They knew that the hard times would soon pass. They just remained prayerful.

CHAPTER 3:

The Lake

Spring was around the corner and the smell of it was in the air. The smell of cow manure, the pigs, and the horse manure to some people was very aromatic because they were looking forward to a good and prosperous spring. The buds were popping out on the trees and berry bushes, clothes were hung out on the clotheslines to dry and going to school was not a problem. Even though life seemed wonderful and full of joy, something else was about to happen. There had been rumors of another war and everybody at the church was talking about it. As it turns out the rumors were true and men were being drafted. Some of the men had excuses not to have to go to war; poor health, a youngest child in the family to keep the family name going, or they had to help on the farm for the rest of the family. David didn't have to go to war because he had to help out with the farm, he considered himself pretty fortunate. Joseph didn't have to go off to war either. Of course, as soon as the boys were of age it was a possibility that they would be drafted. Most of the young men were afraid because they had seen other veterans either die or come home with broken legs, arms or worse. Uncle Teddy lost both of his legs in the war and he needed continuous care at home but he didn't give up the fight. He still had a good heart though, he even adopted one of the children to take care of even though he needed to be taken care of himself. Most of the boys were too young to be drafted, but after the war was over a few of them joined the army anyway. The war was a big dilemma for the poor black farmers along with many obstacles they had already faced. They stayed on their knees praying to God as often as possible.

After a good night's rest and a good weekend it was time to go back to school. Ring!!! School opened and Mr. Phillips began by asking the students if they felt they were experienced enough to plant vegetables and other plants? The whole class said yes! Then the teacher assured them that they would not have to experiment with planting. "Whew! We got out of that one," sighed the children. "We will go straight into health class since the school year is practically over, we need to at least touch this subject so that you will know what to do this summer if you get ill or have an accident. We will begin with reading Chapter 10 of our health books. Girls and boys make sure you read pages 220 through 225 about hygiene because more than likely you will have a short quiz on this section of the chapter. After we have studied this lesson together, a test will be given. I will check to see which group has the most correct answers. The group with the most correct answers will receive a gift. The group with the least correct answers will have to take another test. Is that clear?" said Mr. Phillips. "Yes, Sir," said the students. At that point, the students were dismissed for the day.

The very next day at school the teacher asked about ten questions pertaining to health and hygiene. The girls answered most of the questions correctly. He gave all of the girls a beautiful gold necklace. The boys felt really bad and at that moment they would have done anything to win the gift. But anyway, it was the end of the year so the teacher did give the boys a watch. The looks on their faces changed dramatically with happiness. This did not exclude them from retaking the test through. At the end of the week the students received their grades. Most of them did pretty good considering everything they had gone through. The dismissal bell rang and the students ran out of the school as fast as they could. For some this would be the last year there, some would go to another school and some would simply call it quits and go on to work.

Mary had already decided that she would go to Woodstock, a residential school for boys and girls. The real reason why she wanted to go to another school was because she could not take the difficulties at home with her mama and daddy. Woodstock was a golden opportunity for her. Daddy George had already promised to pay for her tuition.

Spring was about to end and summer was fast approaching, temperatures had already reached the one hundred degree mark, so it was obvious that it was going to be a very hot summer. It seemed even hotter when working in the fields planting the crops. All the students could think about was the fun they were going to have swimming in the lake, fishing, and going on boat rides. They were happy as little larks. It was the middle of May and the raspberries were very beautiful because the weather had been just right for them. Some of the children were afraid to go out and pick berries because the snakes in the field were just waiting to eat the insects and take a bite of anything that was in the way. Papa George said that snakes only eat things that they kill. When the berries were picked and cleaned everybody took some of them home and had a pie baking good time. The apples were not ready yet but as soon as they were ripe, someone was ready to bake a pie. When the peaches were ripe they really baked a slew of pies. Mama Julia loved her peach trees. Mama Julia's peach trees bloomed late in the summer and if she or anyone that wanted to bake a pie missed the day they were ripe, they were not going to get to make a pie. The peaches went away just that fast.

Fishing was a special sport for Joseph, David, John and Samuel because they loved to catch fish, take them home, clean them and cook them. They usually caught huge fish: buffalo, cat fish and crappie. They even caught a couple of turtles and cooked them for dinner. Not very many people ate turtle meat, but the ones that tried seemed to like it very much.

After the farming was done, the days started to appear extremely hot and humid. Everybody complained about how hot it was and wanted to move north at that very moment to keep cool. Even though it was hot they still walked to church every Sunday. Paper fans were quite a commodity and they were used quite often as sweat poured from their faces. They continually wiped their faces with handmade handkerchiefs. Some of the ladies' handkerchiefs were made of cotton lace and they were very delicate and pretty. Most of the girls wouldn't even think of not having their fancy handkerchiefs with them on Sunday.

The preacher spoke about John the Baptist one day and how many people he had baptized. The congregation learned that John the Baptist even baptized Jesus who happened to be his cousin. This was very interesting to the children. The whole church was just about ready to go out and get baptized after hearing the bible story. After church was over everybody went home and got some lemon aid and chopped up some ice and quickly found a shade tree to sit under, because it had been a long hot day.

The crops were looking beautiful including the corn, the green beans, the lima beans, the tomatoes, the potatoes and the cabbage. Some of the crops would have to be picked soon so that they could be sold immediately during the summer months. If they didn't get the corn quickly, all of the some of the little critters in the field would eat them up completely. Sometimes while picking the cotton, Mary and Thomas would sneak off in the woods to find snakes to kill. It was fun, as far as they were concerned, to chop off the heads of the snakes with the hoe that they used when tilling the garden. Then they would hang them on a tree branch. The snakes were really out and mean during the mating season, but any other time the snakes usually moved on about their business. Later in the evening the children would go home and discuss with the family what they did in the fields that day. "Mama Josephine! Did you know Mary was out there killing snakes with the garden hoe," Paul would say. "No, I didn't," said Mama. "No, Mama Josephine that was Thomas out there killing snakes, not me," yelled Mary. "Don't ya'll know you could get bit and die with a snake bite? Leave them snakes alone. I mean that cause there ain't no doctors close by and I don't know what to do about cutting out no snake bites. There is a little warm water in there with some soap, now gwoin and wash up," Mama hollered. "Yes, Mama Josephine," said the children.

The children were running out of things to do to keep the summer fun and excitement. It was getting so hot that everybody would just go down to the lake and jump in it. The whole neighborhood would go to the lake to cool off in the summer. It was enjoyment for everyone including the elderly people. They tied ropes to the trees so that they could swing across the lake and rope in it if they wanted to. The girls were very shy at times because when their clothes were wet, of course every bump and curve would show. The boys didn't care one way or the other.

"Hey Mary, catch hold to the rope and swing across the lake," said Dave. "I ain't gonna swing across no lake on a rope," Mary responded. "Aw, you ain't no fun," said Dave. Mary turned to Valerie and Martha and said, "what in the world is wrong with him? He must be half way out of his mind to be thankin that I'm gonna swing across the lake." "Hey, Valerie show that child how to swing across the lake, would ya?" said Dave. Valerie replied with, "Dave, why did you call her a child as if she was dumb or something when you know that is not true?" "Well she act like she can't even swing on a rope," said Dave. "Why don't you come over here yourself and show her how to swing across the lake," said Valerie. "Alright, I'll be right over there," said Dave. John looked as if to say man what are you getting yoself into. Dave replied in his usual way, "aw nothin." He came to the other side and showed Mary how to hold the rope and rap your feet around the lower part. Somehow he rapped himself around the rope also and before Mary could say, "let me off this rope." They were swinging across the lake and both of them went sliding off into the water with a splash. Everybody turned around and began to laugh. Mary was very upset and Dave thought it was very exciting. Valerie and Martha ran to Mary's rescue and rapped a blanket around her because she was shivering. Mary was so embarrassed that she decided to go home and didn't come out for several days.

Later that evening as Dave and all of the other boys were still swimming in the lake, a startling thing happened. They were practicing their dives into the bottom of the lake, when Dave sensed that something wasn't quite right. He began to move very slowly and cautiously when he came upon a still body in the water. He yelled at the top of his lungs for the rest of the boys to come and witness what he saw in the water. Neither one had an answer as to what they should do, because they knew that they would be interrogated to the hundredth degree. They went to the preacher who then called the city morgue to remove the body from the lake.

They learned after the investigation that the body was that of old man Albert. They could not determine why this man was in the lake nor could they determine if he had fallen in the water accidentally or if it was intentional foul play.

The death of old man Albert was very sad and the rest of the summer would not be the same as the summers before. He was a very friendly man and he would do anything he could to help someone in need. His funeral was a few days later at the church. It was a sad funeral and he only had about two family members left in his immediate family. Nobody knew of anybody else in his family. There was so much negative talk about the incident at the Lake, that after that no one was interested in going there to swim any more. It didn't stop the younger children from going around there to play. Some would go and just run around the Lake and look at the turtles, frogs and snakes crawling around and they would occasionally take one home. Some of the people made fishing rods and went fishing more often but no one went swimming for a very long time. Some of the people made boats and paddles and went for short boat rides.

The children's mothers prayed long and hard about the Lake incident. They prayed that someone would find out what happened to old man Albert and that nothing would happen to their own children at the Lake during the summer or any other time for that matter. The children were getting older and most of them were teen aged children now and wanted to expand their horizons such as having the opportunity to go horseback riding in other parts of the town.

John and Samuel were now about sixteen and seventeen and they wanted to go out on dates with the girls. One day they planned to ask their parents if they could go out on a date. "Mama and Dad, can we saddle up the horses and go pick up Peggy and Joline," asked John. Daddy Samuel politely stood up and put his pipe to his mouth while he pulled on his suspenders and asked in a firm tone of voice, "where in the world are you going time time of the night on horses?" "Well we were hopin we could go to the barn dance and the picture show," replied the boys. "Don't rightly know about that boys, it's kind of rough goin that way this time of night." "Aw pa, it ain't that bad, we will be extra careful with the horses and make sure no one gets hurt," said the boys. "Well, I reckon you boys can go, but don't go too far out yonder cause it is goin to be awful late here in da reckly. Don't you boys let nothin happen to those gurls and those horses cause I sho don't want those mamas fussin at me bout nothing, ya hear me?" said Daddy Samuel. "Yes sir," said the boys and off they flew. The boys went to pick up the girls and of course the girls were not ready yet because their ma and pa had to talk to them before they left the house.

Mr. Baker was very strict about his girls going out at night especially with boys. He stood up and walked the girls to the door and said, "remember what I told you girls, now don't you do anything that I told you not to do, ya hear me," said Mr. Baker. "Yes sir," replied the girls.

Finally they were off to their destination. First they went off a piece by the Lake as the big bright orange sun was setting, to watch the frogs leaping around the yard and there were even a few turtles. They talked about going back to school and what they wanted to see and do when they grew up. Neither one of them really had any idea what they wanted to do, they just knew they wanted to leave the little town, get a job and live the American Dream.

They got back on their horses and galloped off to the barn dance. Everybody was there because they hadn't had much fun since the incident at the Lake. Some of the girls from down yonder were wondering why the two Strong boys, John and Samuel picked up Peggy and Joline instead of them. Martha and Margie went over to the boys and said "umph, we seen ya'll down by the Lake on our way over here, what was ya'll doin over there for?" The boys said, "it ain't none of ya'lls business what we was doin." "Come on Margie let's tell everybody that we saw them down by the Lake," said Martha. "Go on and tell it, we wasn't doin nothing wrong anyway and we don't care if you tell cause you don't know what ya talking bout anyway," said John. "Well ya know ya ain't supposed to be down by that Lake anyhow, especially since that man was found dead," Margie replied. "Aw shut up, ain't nobody at that Lake now," said Samuel. "Come on ya'll let's do the jitta bug. Hey, yeah everybody dance," yelled the youngsters.

They were having a good time when all of a sudden their teacher, Mr. Phillips walked in to see how they were doing. He had a drink or two and ended up dancing just as much as the children. Mr. Phillips apparently missed seeing his children at school and he was ready to get started again. Of course, some of the children were leaving the old school the teacher wanted to visit with them for just a little while to see if they had any idea what was ahead and what they planned to do with the rest of their lives. A light came on in Mr. Phillips's mind as he thought to himself that telling about their summers would be a good first assignment for the students returning to school in a few weeks as August was about to be over. Obviously, the students didn't want to discuss the subject of school so everyone continued to have a wonderful time. Martha asked Mr. Phillips to dance and to her surprise he could just as good as she could.

It was getting late and very dark outside, so Peggy and Joline reminded John and Samuel that it was time for them to go home before their pa would came looking for them. They thanked God for the stars, the moon and the light that they gave at night because it was really dark outside. Some people adjust very well to the dark and that is how John and Samuel found their way to the girls' house that night. As they were on their way home they went by the Lake again.

Since their eyes had adjusted to the darkness, they could see figures and all four of them saw a figure running through the trees around the Lake and it frightened them something fierce. John clicked for his horse to pick up the speed and Samuel was not far behind. The girls screamed all the way home. No one said anything else about the Lake that night. They saw a little light in the house, pa had left the lantern lit for them.

When the boys got home, a lantern was still lit also. Everybody was asleep, but the wind began to blow very hard. Suddenly a storm was brewing and the wind was so fierce that it knocked down a few very small trees. The cows and pigs began to stir around and the chickens were flying around. John and Samuel had to go right back outside and gather the pigs because they were trying to get away. David and pa went to check on the cows which were a little further out from the house. About four of them were missing. Hopefully they would come back in the morning. Also some of the crops were damaged. Even though the storm ripped through the town and destroyed homes and crops, everyone still had confidence and was optimistic that everything would be alright. Sure enough, it wasn't very long before things were back to normal after a few months.

Later that summer, the lake was purchased by the county and they changed a few rules. No one was allowed to swim in it anymore, but the people could use it as a fishing ground and picnic area. This was quite alright with most of the people in the town.

It wasn't long before summer was over. Most of the children really weren't ready for summer to end. The older boys had already graduated or just left school. There were still some children going to the old Strong family school house in the fifties, not very many though. Sometimes one or two students were in the classroom, but classes still resumed. The teacher didn't mind as long as he had someone to teach.

Time to get ready to go back to school and hit the books since time was drawing nigh. Mary had transferred to Woodstock. Her teachers wore those old funny looking shoes, but they were well made. Mary met many girls her age and at times she even enjoyed herself. Although the environment was much better at Woodstock, Mary missed her sister and brothers and she became so depressed that her grades began to fall. She called her aunt all of the time asking her to send money. Mary's aunt began to wonder what she was doing with the money. Not willing to accept the crumbling grades and the depression, Mary decided that she would leave Tennessee altogether and go to Chicago, IL. Daddy George's sister lived in Chicago and she worked in a laundry. Mary was around seventeen years old when she moved to Chicago. She did not go back to school although she only needed one year to graduate. David, the boy that Mary liked even though she him to be obnoxious at times, had already taken a job in Chicago before Mary moved there. It seemed as though this would be the answer for her. David wanted to simply learn about other places, other than his home town and he was kind of tired of living on his father's farm even though his father made him earn his keep.

While Mary was living in Chicago, a young man proposed to her. His name was Charlie Murphy. Mary accepted the proposal. Her aunt didn't think it was time to have a wedding after all she was only seventeen. It was not unheard of to get married at seventeen or even a couple years younger. Mary was so young and her friends thought that she wanted to get married just to get out on her own. Everyone began to think that this was more than likely for convenience rather than love because Mary was really not interested and certainly not in love with Charlie. She thought long and hard about this and came to her senses and she broke off the engagement. After all, she found out that David was still single and living not far from her in the same city.

Mary tried desperately to continue her single life and just work and maybe go back to school. Aunt Elsie was a plain drunk. She was as nice and sweet as she could be, but she had a slight condition called alcoholism that changed her personality completely. Her husband, Ralph, didn't help the situation very much. Aunt Elsie drank, drank and drank until she could barely walk down the sidewalk without someone making comments about her and laughing at her while she tried to walk. One day when she was going to the store, a couple young boys yelled out, "Hey old drunk lady where do you think you are going?" Then they roared with laughter. She replied slurring and slobbering all over herself, "I ain't no old drunk lady and get you some business." Aunt Elsie denied that she was an alcoholic, but there was no way she could hide this serious condition.

Mary was very embarrassed by this and could barely stand living with her Aunt anymore, but she remembered how hard it was when she was living in Tennessee and decided to try and stick it out. One night when Mary was out with some of her coworkers, she saw David and Angelo out on the town. They got together that night and had a good time laughing about how ironic it was that both of them wound up in Chicago. They called each other on a regular basis and it was not long before David and Mary were talking about getting married.

David was twenty-five years old and had experienced just a little bit more than Mary but even though Mary was much younger, she could cook up a meal that would make David come back for seconds and thirds. She was also very particular about her clothes and her appearance since she was in the laundry business at that time. It was beginning to seem that they were destined to live in Chicago for the duration. They went to the Justice of the Peace on October 31, 1953 and were married in a blink of the eye. A big reception was held afterwards and many of their relatives were there. Some of them already lived in Chicago.

Ma Mary and Pa David

Living in Chicago was good for a little while for David and Mary. They were not accustomed to the below zero degree weather and deep snow that kept them shut in for days at a time and the job situation was not stable for David. He wanted to work for the railroad, but that just didn't happen for him. David's friend, Angelo, had a pretty good job and he kept plenty of money even though he lived lavishly and he dressed real flashy. Angelo suffered with substance abuse. He also drank like a fish and stayed loaded with alcohol. Unfortunately, the effects of the drugs and alcohol eventually took him away from this world. Mary and David reluctantly accepted what happened to their best friend and tried to get on with their lives the best way they knew how.

David and Mary made the decision to move back to Tennessee to work on the farm and live in a very tiny house that he built with own two hands. About three weeks after they moved back to Tennessee, Mary realized that something different was happening with her body. She soon learned that she was going to have a baby. Not only was she going to have a baby, but she was having some difficulty carrying the baby as she did with her second child. She threatened a miscarriage and they went back to Chicago to a Japanese doctor and he was able to save her and her baby. Mary went back to Tennessee and delivered their baby at the hospital where just about everybody that had a baby that year went to have their baby. Their second baby girl was born premature in Memphis, TN. While Mary was in the hospital delivering the baby she began to holler and scream frantically because the pain was unbearable. A Caucasian nurse came to calm her down but instead, she offended Mary.

After Mary delivered her baby, she remembered that the nurse had been inhospitable. Mary thought the nurse to be very rude and she didn't want to repeat the words that came out of the nurse's mouth. Mama Josephine was so upset that Mary was treated badly that she made her repeat what the nurse said to her. Mary said that the nurse said, "aw go on and have that little "n" word baby." This upset everybody in the room and needless to say that back in 1955, some ugly, dirty words were left on the wall of that room that were directed to the nurse. They went home to their little log house in the country about 35 miles away. Thank goodness it was in the spring or they wouldn't have been able to keep warm in their poorly insulated house, with no running water and no inside bathroom. Life had not changed much in the country since they had moved away and moved back home again.

Baby food was always prepared at home like it is for most people in the twenty-first century. Thank goodness for goats milk on the farm because it helped to keep Mary's little baby girls healthy. The second baby really needed more milk because she had weak bones.

Farming was still about the same as it was years ago and it was not certain that enough money would come from the crops to pay for the farm, the taxes plus their other living expenses.

The pressure was on David to provide for his family and take care of the farm and it had gotten to be a bit much. Besides being upset with the way things were going with the family and some of the negative things that were said about his marriage, David was just plain fed up with the way his family was being treated. Sometimes the pressure was so bad that even his family was intolerable. Some days would get downright miserable.

Along with financial and family disagreements at times one would have thought that David's family was extremely color struck. His family would talk about his dark skinned children. Mary was very sensitive when she even thought that someone was talking about her children behind their backs. David was very sensitive as well because he was not in the least bit color struck even though his skin underneath his clothes was as white as any Caucasian person. He tanned very easily especially after working in the field. His brother Joseph was a little darker and David would do anything he could for his brother. He even helped him leave Tennessee when he was believed to be in trouble with the law.

Word spread quickly that jobs were plentiful in a small town in Ohio about 700 miles away from Chicago. David went to work while Mary stayed on the farm until he sent for her. When he found an apartment for his family, he immediately sent for them. This was his children's first train ride. Ohio was also where David's three sisters lived. He loved his eldest sister, Hanna, dearly. Naturally, he couldn't pass up the thought of living close to her. David and Mary packed up their belongings and started their journey. When David and Mary arrived, his second oldest sister, Agnes, offered a room to live in until they got on their feet and could afford a place of their own. The house was very nice considering the year it was built. It had inside restrooms, bathrooms and rooms upstairs which they did not hesitate to offer David and Mary. David went to work every day and Mary took care of their two little girls. Everything was going well in the little town while the jobs were stable, but as soon as David and Leonard were out of a job, depression set in and they wondered where they would get their next meal to feed their families. While they were unemployed, Leonard and David did little odd jobs such as repairing houses, plumbing, roofing, cracked sidewalks, painting, building houses and even loading/hauling garbage for businesses and private homes. They did practically any job offered to make ends meet at home for their families.

Train station like the one Mama Mary and Papa
David boarded for Ohio back in 1955

At times it was just devastating what they had to do for a living, especially when hauling trash to and from places. To make the reality of poverty bearable, sometimes they reverted back to the old standby money making method and that was making liquor (bootlegging moonshine) but they would end up drinking it too. This habit didn't help their depression and frustration. None of their wives approved of their drinking and it caused many domestic quarrels at home. Mary tried her best to fight with David about this but he was so tall over her that the fight would end before it ever started. "Dave that is not fair, but you better believe I will hit you back," said Mary. Then she would either drown her frustrations out by cooking, crying or praying to God that this bad habit would end soon. By the next morning everything would be back to normal as if nothing had every happened.

Since David loved hunting, he had several dogs to feed as well as his family. He had a bird dog, a beetle dog and several hound dogs. At first, the neighbors couldn't stand the howling but since the town was extremely quiet, it soon became a welcomed sound. The dogs always let them know when someone was prowling around. One night one of the dogs freed itself from the dog pin and a truck came by and ran over her. It squashed her so badly that it made her have a bowel movement. Everybody ran to see what the noise was all about. It was so bad to see that the bird dog "Lady" died so tragically. Everybody loved Lady, even though Mary thought David gave the dogs too much attention. One of his hound dogs was later found dead under the house. David told his young girls that the dog was struck by lightning.

The time had come for the third child, Dave was finally working another job and they had their own little house not far from David's other sister Albertina and her husband Ned. Mary was excited about her new home and another baby on the way. They were hoping that this particular child would finally be a boy since they already had two little girls. All of Dave's sisters and brothers had boys. It was beginning to be a family joke that David didn't have any boys, but he loved his girls just the same.

Since everything was going good, the men wanted to be entertained to keep life from being so monotonous. The small city had baseball games, the cafes, the gambling halls, and the dance clubs to entertain them. Well along with entertainment came the booze, the women, the smoking and the creeping out with other people other than their spouses. The town was running over with prosperity. So much that even David's other two brothers came to Ohio to work. With all of this entertainment, Hanna began to wonder what was going to happen now that there was so much action in the town. She began to go to church more often and prayed more often just as her Mama Julia did when they were growing up.

A new bar opened up called the Highland Café and the men got together and decided to go to the Café` that one of the black men in the city decided to open. It was the hottest Café` in town. Everybody went there for entertainment and liquor. It was only natural to buy liquor, listen to the music, and talk with the other guys. For some unknown reason there was one fellow in the Café that had a problem with David. He was what they called a "city slicker." Apparently, this city slicker didn't like David's actions. No one really knew why he had a problem with David. He walked around the room a couple of times, smoked a cigar, and played cards. Finally, he came closer to David and his two brothers, John and Samuel. Then out of nowhere, he pulled a pistol on them and began shooting. Sadly, David was shot. Quickly, John and Samuel pulled out an army gun and shot the "city slicker." Both of them were alive and were rushed to the hospital where they were treated for their wounds.

When Mary was told about the terrible incident, she was terrified and began to scream and holler all over the place and soon after that she went into a state of shock. They called the doctor and he had to give her a sedative. David was Mary's life and to lose him would be like losing herself. As far as she was concerned, nothing could take the place of him. Mary was very depressed while carrying their third child. She wondered what she should do and how would she make it in this world. They had very little money but they still had to eat and pay bills. Thank God she had some family in town to help with food and other necessities. The other two children were too young to go to school, so Mary didn't have to worry about them not getting enough days in school for the year. Neither David nor Mary knew how they were going to handle a new baby in September since David was not able to work at that time. Thanks be unto God, they were able to get into the hospital to deliver the third baby. The whole family pitched in to help pay for the delivery.

Dave was still very angry about his condition and anxiety would get the best of him because he couldn't move around the same way he used to. His accident changed him tremendously because the bullet was still lodged next to his spinal cord. He had to take all kinds of medicine and he couldn't drink booze like he used to. Every now and then his anxieties would get the best of him so the doctor prescribed tranquilizers to calm him down. The tranquilizers seemed to work pretty well. Dave was able to go back to work and pay bills and still have a little savings account.

Dave worked and dedicated himself to his family and stayed away from the cafés for the most part. After Dave regained most of his strength he decided to build a house by using the skill that he acquired when working with his brother-in-law. The town seemed to be making progress at the time even though there was a lot of undeveloped property and people would come and people would go. Old depreciated houses were torn down and the property would stay vacant, leaving the town kind of empty. The house that David built was not large at all, but it was big enough for the time being and they could at least take a nice bath with running water. It was unlike the house that they were used to in the country. Everything was going fine and they loved their little house. The neighbors had a huge house and the house seemed very dark sometimes. It looked as if it had been there for many, many ears. The neighbors made Dave and Mary feel so welcome when they moved into their house. Dave and Mary were always invited to their home.

Mary was expecting yet another baby. This would be their fourth child. The family sympathized with her and teased Dave for having all girls again and even after they thought all of the teasing was over, another girl was born. So what else could Dave's sisters and brothers do but tease him again. At first, Dave didn't quite know how to deal with it. He slowly began drinking and smoking again. These two vices were in Dave's system. He tried desperately to quit. Mary prayed for him constantly, she confided in his eldest sister, she called the preacher to house to pray for him and she would take the cigarettes and alcohol from him. He still continued on in his own merry way. "They can't tell me what to do, but I love you all," he would say. He was just a happy go lucky man and he was very blessed even though wondered if he was aware of it. Sometimes he would even get up early on Sunday and go to church. He always paid his respects at funerals and he had a pretty good idea as to how he was still getting around on this old earth.

Even though Dave was a happy man, sometimes he would get depressed about this and that. Nobody ever knew what he was so depressed about because he didn't talk a whole lot. Mary told him that he needed to let all of that bottled up stuff come out sometimes and that the only time he talked was when he had been drinking. Dave felt that he should only talk when he really needed to and when he did talk it was almost always in a low smooth tone, never extremely loud. He said what he wanted to say and went on about his business as if he hadn't said a word. Sometimes he talked as if he was talking only to himself. That was what was so good about him, he had a great deal of humility and he was proud at the same time. Even though he went out and had a good time with the boys he was very humble and you couldn't help but to love him.

Drawing of Papa David working

While the Strong boys were in Ohio trying to build a life, have a home and take care of their families, life was still going on in Tennessee. Grandpa Samuel and Grandma Julia were still farming and living in a small house on the farm in the same place near Blueberry Hill. Of course, their children would come home every now and then to visit them. It was always a wonderful occasion, even though there was a big difference from the way the children were living now. Grandma and grandpa were still pumping water from a pump in the ground in front of the house. Sometimes they would draw water from the water well. They called it "well water." It was home to the children, to the grandchildren it was an antique world that they were not used to although they had so much fun they forgot about their grandparents' old-fashioned way. The grandchildren had learned a song in school that said "over the river and through the woods to grandmother's house we go" and they sang that song every time they went to Mama Julia's house. Grandma and grandpa considered themselves blessed to have what they had and that was all they wanted.

As the young became old, the old became older and weaker and unable to do the things that they used to do. Mary's grandmother, Mama Tena fell ill and even though she could not help around the house, thank God the people that she worked for allowed her to stay with them in her own little house on the same property. It was very hard to accept the fact that Mama Tena was so ill because she had been such a strong lady all of her life. She used to carry everything on top of her head no matter what it was. People in the area said that her employers were very kind to her. Although Mr. Albert was very ill as well, he still took care of Mama Tena. Supposedly Mama Tena had children by Mr. Albert and it was a well kept secret. Mama Tena named all of her children after another man that she worked for even though two of her children were certainly Mr. Albert Brandberry's children.

The teacher, Mr. Phillips, would stop by to check on Mr. Albert and his sister every now and then and if they needed something cooked, he would cook for them too. Eventually, Mr. Albert died and Mama Tena was still in the little house that he gave her. Her sons George, James and Ray would come by to see how she was doing every now and then.

There was a rumor that the teacher, Mr. Phillips had come into a lot of money but nobody knew how it happened. It was a little bit suspicious since Mr. Albert had just died and Ms. Annette was sick and would let Mr. Phillips come to the house anytime he wanted to even though he had a family of his own. Mr. Albert's body was transported to England and he was buried there. Anyway when Mr. Phillips came into this money, he didn't give any to his family or friends. He just put it in a suitcase and went to Ohio to visit David, Hanna, Agnes and Albertina since they were all students and relatives of his at one point and time. When he showed them all of that money, they wondered where he got it and why was he carrying it around like that. People were saying that he was so tight with his money that he may have actually saved that much. After his visit to Ohio, he went back home and there was talk around town that his "mind had gone bad" and he was so very ill to the point that he died. What he did with all of that money, nobody knew. For all they knew it may still be buried somewhere out in the field. After this happened, Mama Tena's health became increasingly worse. Nobody really knew what made her so ill. There was some speculation that she had rheumatic arthritis or maybe it was just old age. Mama Tena died of a long illness but nobody wanted to keep the house, so it was given to someone in Mr. Albert's family.

Mr. Phillips in his classroom at the schoolhouse

Since the enrollment at the old Strong school was lower than ever before, the county made the decision to sell the school. Many people in the area wanted to keep the school as it was, but the county just could not keep it going. Many people wanted to purchase the old school because of it had a history. Grandpa Samuel decided that since the land belonged to Fannie and David Strong and the school was named after them, why not try to buy it back from the school system. He really didn't have much money to buy the old school especially at that time but he worked hard and earned enough to put a down payment on the total amount of the school. Grandma Julia and Grandpa Samuel were excited about buying the old schoolhouse.

It really meant something to them and they knew that it was going to be a very special place for all of the Strong family, relatives and friends. They were right. It was a very special place for the family to visit at vacation time. Even though it was very hot in the summertime and very cold in the winter, when you went home somehow those things just didn't matter anymore. Even though they didn't have inside running water at first or electricity, the warmth and light was inside the house.

Grandma Julia always cooked breakfast in the morning, she loved going out to her chicken house to get fresh eggs, and she loved cooking homemade biscuits. Everything was going just fine but suddenly prices started to go up and the money was at the lowest point it could possible go. The crops were not as good and the farm animals were not as plentiful. It got to the point that the only thing Grandpa Samuel could think to do was to sell some of his land in order to keep the old schoolhouse. So that is just what he did.

They lived in the schoolhouse comfortably after selling part of the land. Some of the other family members, cousins, second cousins, uncles and aunts, felt that they didn't really need to sell any of their land but Grandpa Samuel knew what he needed to do and he didn't let them tell him what to do about anything. Grandma and Grandpa Samuel kept many of the books from the schoolhouse and they even tried to read and understand them. This helped them very much even though they had plenty of good common sense and prayed every day. The more they tried to read, the more knowledgeable they became. Everyone wondered how they did so well, living like they did without formal education and the relatives wondered how they managed without all of the up-to-date things that most people had at that time. They simply depended on God to lead and guide them through everything they did.

Grandma and Grandpa Samuel became so settled in their house which used to be a school that they decided not to sell another piece of property to anyone else. They had no thoughts of anyone selling the home that they called the family home. When the children came home to visit, it was always a wonderful occasion. They still drove on dirt roads to the country store. They still used the black pot bellied stove for heat and they were still happy with everything thing they had.

The people that bought the piece of land that Grandpa sold to them just adored being there in their new home. The time seemed to fly by after Grandpa and Grandma were settled into their schoolhouse home. The children weren't getting any younger. Many of the older grandchildren graduated from school and had already started making lives for themselves. The oldest grandchild named Joshua went on to the army. This was Grandma Julia's eldest child's son. So many grandchildren were graduating at the same time that grandma and grandpa couldn't keep up with them all. Forget getting a graduation gift if you didn't come home to get it. Grandma Julia still made her quilts and pudding cakes and if you got one as a gift, you were considered very fortunate.

Even though all of the children thought about "home" often, the reality was that they had made their homes in Ohio. The people were basically very friendly in Ohio, but the times were Changing and they were changing very fast. The little town in Ohio seemed to be just as productive as its surroundings sounds in some areas.

The younger children went to school daily, year round except for the summer break. Not like their parents who went to school as long as they weren't home working on the farm. The schools were much bigger than the schoolhouse that their parents attended some years ago. The homework was different also. The math changed and sometimes the parents simply could not help their children with their homework. Things had changed so much in the fifties and early sixties. Many of the children's teachers in Ohio were Caucasian and proper grammar was very important. Some of the parents went to school and had proper speaking teachers, but the parents still had the black southern accents. The children would come home from school speaking with a

European tone and their parents thought they were mocking someone, but that was the way the children were being taught to speak.

The southern children were often ridiculed and criticized by other northern blacks as well as the northern whites about their southern accents. This gave the southern sounding children sort of an inferiority complex about their southern accents. They felt that their speech was inadequate and some of them became withdrawn in the classroom and felt that other students were making fun of them. It was a different story when they left the school and went home or out on the playground where they released their thoughts and voiced their opinions. Sometimes the teachers stood around and listened carefully. Sometimes it was very funny to the children to hear the different accents and as time went on the people finally became more accustomed with the different sounds. Elizabeth loved to go to school and read when she got home from school. All of the other girls usually found time to play instead of read. Mama Mary often needed Elizabeth's help in the evenings. Mama Mary would call out for Elizabeth several times in one day. Elizabeth would get tired of her calling sometimes and act as though she didn't hear her calling. Finally Mama Mary would say, "Hey Black Mattie, didn't you hear me calling you?" The other girls would fall out laughing and start mocking Mama Mary by saying, "Hey Black Mattie." It was so funny that even Elizabeth had to laugh.

Going to school was exciting for some of the children and they wanted to play and have fun most of the time. But the teachers were strict up north and if the students didn't get their lessons, they failed that grade which was unlike the one room schoolhouse. One of the strictest teachers was Ms. Elliott. She was a very precise teacher and it seemed as though she didn't have another life besides teaching school. She taught all of the children how to tell time. She would say, "alright class we are going to make a clock. Draw a circle on your cardboard and number it up to 12:00 and then I want you to put the gold fastener in the center of the circle. Now spread the prongs out flat on the circle. See how the hands move around the clock." "Yes, Ms. Elliott," said the children. "Now I want each of you to show me where 2:00 is on the circle and raise it up in the air when you are finished, so that I can see all of them. Is everybody done?" "Yes, Ms. Elliott." "Oh! Rodney, you did not put the hands on 2:00 like I asked you. Now put it on 3:00 since you did not get it right on 2:00." "Yes, Ms. Elliott." Rodney could not get the time correct for anything in the world. Ms. Elliott seemed to become frustrated with him, but she continued to work with him the best she could until he finally learned to tell time.

"I told you Ms. Elliott was the strictest teacher in the whole school, said Betty. So why didn't you listen to me, Rodney?" "Aw, I ain't got time to sit down and make hands move on a circle," said Rodney. "I don't know why not, you got time to go out and run around to your friend's house. All I got say is you'd better learn your lesson," said Betty.

One good thing about the teachers in the north, they did care about the students on a personal level as well as an educational level. If a student could not get to school, the teacher would do everything within her power to get the student to school. If the student didn't have clothes, the teacher would try to find clothes for them. The teachers often wanted to know if everything was alright at home. They didn't want the children to have unnecessary stress even though most of them had family crises anyway and this was something that the teachers realized. That they were going to have to take everything into consideration when teaching.

The teachers tried to keep up with each generation of children. Some of the teachers tried to compare siblings in certain families. Sometimes this didn't help the younger siblings, especially when the eldest sibling had left a good impression on the teacher. One generation of children was so nice to their new black teacher and she loved students that particular year. But, when the third generation of children entered into her classroom some changes had to be made because of the cutoff age, so the teacher had to put two different age groups in one classroom. It was almost unbearable for the teacher because of the differences in the class.

The children didn't care about doing their work and didn't respect the new black teacher as much as they respected the other teachers. One day the teacher just broke down and cried in the classroom. "You are the worse group of children I have ever had," said Mrs. Greeney.

The children did not stop acting up, they just started laughing at her. For one thing, they had never seen a teacher wearing contacts.

One day, one of her contacts fell out on the floor and the teacher panicked. "Don't move, I gotta find my contact, so don't move," repeated the teacher. The children filled the classroom with laughter and from then on, the teacher had a hard time with the students. Even though some of the students were bad, the teacher tried very hard to keep up with them as they moved on to another level. She was always willing to give good advice whenever it was necessary.

It was not uncommon to see black children walking home with white children in the late sixties in the north. It was not uncommon to see them playing with each other at one another's house, listening to one another's music, riding each others' horses and simply having plain old fun in each other's yards. On the other hand some of the whites and blacks wouldn't even think of visiting another race or listening to their music, it was something they just didn't do. The children knew who would associate with them and who would not associate with them.

Walking to school with schoolmates was fun for Dave and Mary's children especially when their parents were not home for lunch. The children would go home and eat lunch, clean up the house, play on the furniture and the highlight of the afternoon was a fighting match. Sometimes the fights would get serious and cause serious pain. Dave and Mary's two eldest children got into a fight every day. They would soon forget about the fights after each one got their swing, in the living room chair that swirled around and around. Then they went back to school as if they had done nothing wrong. The never thought about locking or unlocking the door. Mary probably left the key with the neighbor and she would let them in for lunch and then lock the door after they left.

"Hey, Strong girls, ya'll better hurry up and come on back to school," said the two Marquette boys, Randy and Gerald. "We're coming," the girls would reply. All of the children would meet up at the same school stop area. When the patrolman blew his whistle, it was time to come in to the school. If the children were not standing around, that meant

everything they were going to get to do for the summer. Fall came and went so quickly. Before anyone could look up the leaves were falling off the trees and everything looked orange, yellow and brown. Mary was not feeling well, but she knew that it was almost time for another child to come into this world.

It was cold and snowy outside when Dave and Mary's last baby was born. Dave was nervous and excited at the same time. They rushed Mary to the hospital and the girls stayed with their neighbor for a couple of days. The girls kind of figured out what was happening with their mother but it was still a surprise when they brought the baby boy home. Everybody fussed over the little bundle of joy because it was a boy. He was spoiled before he could even say mama or daddy. Each girl wanted to hold the baby. "Mama may I hold him," asked the oldest girl. "O.K., but make sure you hold the back of his head." "Mama what's wrong with his eyes? They look like they are going around and around in his head," said the oldest daughter." "He's O.K., many babies do that, it's not abnormal," said Mama. "Well, it looks strange to me," the daughter said. Everybody got a chance to hold the baby then they took him and put him to bed. The girls couldn't get enough of looking at him so they kept going in the bedroom just to get a peep at him. Finally Mary said, "Go and change his diaper." Elizabeth was excited that she was chosen to do the honor. She went to change him and the first thing the baby boy did when she took the old dirty diaper off was to pee in her face. She hollered to Mama and everybody snickered, but she went on and changed him anyway.

Mama Mary was still weak from the delivery because she lost a lot of blood and had to have a blood transfusion which was very dangerous. Mary asked that they give her a hysterectomy but the doctor would not allow her to do that. She wanted no more children after the baby boy was born. Plus, she said that Dave promised her a bigger house or a strand of pearls if this child was boy. Mary reminded him of this promise just about every day for about five or six years. They really needed a bigger house now that they had five children. They had two small bedrooms, one for all four girls and one for the parents and the baby, a very small living room, a small kitchen with a small utility room, but since the girls were still small they weren't concerned about having a lot of space. They were still a little bit happy with their house. Dave later added another room and a kitchen thinking this would be sufficient, but it wasn't.

Dave's sister, Hanna had seven children so she knew she needed a bigger house. They moved into a nice sized home with bathroom and three bedrooms a living room and an eat-in kitchen. Albertina already had a nice sized house but it was old and when she had two more girls they decided to add to their old house only they used the attic.

After a few months had passed, Dave's son from Tennessee who was now in his twenties came to live with them and they immediately realized that they needed much more room than they had at that time. This was a son that the girls knew nothing about and Mary had kind of figured that he had a son somewhere but she was not for sure. The girls really enjoyed having an older brother because he always tried to give them something when he came home from work. The girls enjoyed these wonderful surprises. Dave's son's name was David, Jr. and of course Dave was very proud of having a son, especially since he had been teased so much for having four girls in a row. When his son came to live with them, Mary and the girls really didn't know what to expect from David, Jr. They just accepted him in their home. One night Dave, Jr. wanted to go out with the boys to a party. Mary didn't really want him to go out with that bunch especially in their new car. He went out that night and came home, but he was a smoker and a drinker and God knows what else. He liked to fascinate the girls with his smoking. He would take a drag from a cigarette and then exhale the smoke into a Pepsi bottle and hold his finger over the opening of the bottle to keep the smoke in the bottle. The girls thought that it was a neat little trick.

Well once again David, Jr. found some friends to go out and party with only this time he rode in his friends' car. They were going down the highway and ran into someone and they were close to the railroad tracks. They had been smoking and drinking and they were very young of age. They also realized that the boys had been drinking quite a bit of cough syrup to give themselves a higher high than what they already were.

The driver was taken to intensive care, the other passenger was taken to intensive care and

David, Jr. was pronounced dead with a broken neck and crushed chest. Unfortunately, it was a very tragic accident. Dave, Mary and the children had all settled in for the night when a loud knock broke the silence of their home.

The policemen came to tell the dreadful news. When they told Dave what happened, all he could say was "it is not so." He could not believe what he was hearing. When the policemen gave the description of David, Jr., Dave had to come to realization that it was true about his son. The girls got out of the bed and started asking questions. "What happened?" they asked. Mary told the girls to get back in bed. Calm down now, sh, sh, sh, sh, sh. She did all she could to calm them down and she tried to put them back to bed. Dave was really in a bewildered state of mind when he heard the news. He just broke down and cried, cried, and cried. Dave had a very difficult time making arrangements for his son's funeral. Thank goodness he had his brothers and sisters there to help him make arrangements. David, Jr.'s remains were flown back to Memphis where his mother, Minnie was waiting to help with the rest of the funeral arrangements.

It was very painful for everyone in the family. The girls stayed home with their neighbor while Dave and Mary traveled to Tennessee, because they had to go to school even though the loss of their brother had an adverse effect on them. Somehow they lived through this tragedy and were able to continue on with their lives. One day the girls were walking from school and a gang of girls were walking behind them making all kinds of degrading remarks about them. The girls tried to ignore the gang of girls but it was almost impossible to ignore them. One of the gang girls said, "I will slap off four of them." When Elizabeth, Carla, Rebecca, and Bobbie heard this they came up with a plan because these girls were tough and really wanted to fight them. The plan was to turn around and kick all of them, put a few fist hits in it and then split up and run like hell until they got home. The plan worked because the girls gave up trying to catch them. Through all of this they still took time out to remember their deceased brother.

It was years before the family would accept the fact that this happened in such a short time period. Dave began to drink moderately which was something that he really did not want to do. He just thought that he was washing away the pain, but it still would not go away. The girls didn't know what to say or do to cheer him up. They tried everything but nothing worked so they decided to let time heal the wounds.

The girls were beginning to blossom into little women. Dave saw that they were growing up and decided that they desperately needed a slightly bigger house. One day Dave was talking to the neighbors across the street and he learned that they were leaving and wanted to sell their property. Dave thought this would be a good opportunity. He purchased the property from the Quaker family. He saved as much money as he could and ordered the supplies and materials to begin building the house.

Dave worked day and night trying to get the house built before the girls were grown enough to move into their own homes. It wasn't easy building a house in his spare time. He would work on the house in the mornings before he went to work and in the evenings when he got off work. Sometimes at night you could see a light moving around in the house as he worked to complete the job. Much praying was going on as he was working on the house because they knew it was hard on him with the bullet still lodged next to his spine and any wrong move could hurt his back. Everybody had a special feeling as the house started going up. This undertaking kept Dave's mind off the tragedy of his son as well as drinking addiction.

The girls continued to go to school and grow and they remained focused on getting their education. Getting an education was drilled into their minds from the beginning of school all through high school. All of the adults in the neighborhood stressed the importance of getting an education. Even though it was not always easy they managed to add a little fun to their daily lives. They dated, went to parties and joined a junior sorority which really kept them busy. They had meetings every week and assignments every day. At first Mary wouldn't let them join the sorority but they begged, pleaded and really cleaned the house. Mary was quite impressed by this and reluctantly decided to let them join if they made it through the initiation, plus she was really sick and tired of them begging and pleading. The girls made it through initiation and joined the sorority.

Of course, when the sorority had functions such as sorority balls and sorority dinners the girls had to invite dates and escorts. Sometimes this posed a problem because some of the girls had dates and some of them did not have dates. Occasionally, the girls had the problem of choosing the same escort which was very hilarious because it stirred quite a ruckus. Elizabeth went out with her boyfriend to one of the sorority functions and after the date she had to wrestle with him to get him off of her. It was truly a struggle because she was all dressed up and here she was wrestling with her escort. During the struggle she lost one of her earrings so she made him look all over the car for it. He was nice enough to stop wrestling with her and took her home. Thank God, she thought to herself. Dave and Mary could hardly accept the idea of the girls dating but they came to the realization that there would be special events that would include escorts. Sometimes Elizabeth's boyfriend would sneak around the house at night. This kept Dave and Mary very busy because they did not want the girls to end up like so many of the other girls at the tender and delicate age.

Mary was a member of a women's club also, which required meetings away from the house. While Mary was at these meetings and Dave was at work, the boys would bring their friends around the house and sit, talk and try to do whatever they could get away with which was not much because Mary would manage to make sure that nothing went on that wasn't supposed to. If she found out that the girls were doing anything wrong even as much as kissing a boy, she would bring out her rifle and she meant to shoot somebody if it was necessary. Carla decided one day to ignore her mother's warnings and Mary called out saying, "girl if you don't get your behind home right now, I am going to shoot that boy." Carla had the nerve to say, "I will be there in a minute." Mama Mary replied with, "in a minute? Did I hear you say, in a minute? Girl I am coming around the corner with my rifle, now get over here now!" "Oh, ouch, I'm coming," replied Carla.

CHAPTER 4:

Family Life For The Grandchildren

Elizabeth tried her best to set an example for the other girls. It was very difficult because the girls had their own minds, agendas and plus they were getting much bigger than she was getting. Of course, the oldest daughter had to go along with some of the ideas of her younger sisters even if they seemed utterly ridiculous. They would tease her and call her the "book worm" and say that she was like an absent minded professor with book sense and no common sense especially if she didn't have her mind set to do what they were doing. Elizabeth's boyfriend was very smart and witty, which was why Mary was very concerned about her daughter going place with him. When they walked home from a dance or sometime even when they walked from school, Mama would ride directly behind them in her car. Everybody could feel the embarrassment that they were feeling as they walked home. All in all the girls were pretty good while in high school. Carla, the second daughter was dating Elizabeth's boyfriend's friend and he was a strange young fellow. He didn't want to go to school and he didn't want to do any kind of work. Carla wanted to go on a date with him but he couldn't afford to take her nor did he have access to a car to take her anywhere. So Carla fixed that and kind of had her dates at school on the sideline.

Elizabeth's boyfriend played football and she was a majorette at the school therefore they saw quite a bit of each other. He bought her all kinds of gifts while he worked at the hotel. He would also hint around about a girl that worked at the hotel also. Elizabeth didn't know if he was trying to make her jealous or if he was sincere about this other girl. He began to talk as if something was going on with them at the hotel where he worked. Elizabeth's boyfriend was good friends with the star football player. They had a dispute one night that turned into a fist fight on the team's bus. Word got back to Elizabeth that it was an awful fight, something that none of these students would ever suspect because these two guys did everything together and they never had disputes.

The story came out one day that Elizabeth's boyfriend had gotten word from someone that his football friend was interested in Elizabeth. When Elizabeth talked to her boyfriend about it, she assured him that she would never do something such as date her boyfriend's best friend. Besides this guy was the boyfriend of her good friend, Vanessa. This guy was also the blood brother of the other guy that was dating Vanessa. Vanessa was in love with two brothers. The oldest brother flirted with Elizabeth all of the time and she couldn't believe that he was serious about Vanessa because he flirted with many high school girls. The younger brother looked at Elizabeth but he never flirted with her, so she couldn't understand why her boyfriend was fighting with him. Elizabeth really did not want to be in a tangled web. Mama Mary used to tease Elizabeth about him and then she nicknamed him "jack rabbit." The girls teased Elizabeth; they called her Black Mattie and her boyfriend Jack Rabbit. Whenever they went out on a date Mama Mary would tell her to keep her underwear up. Elizabeth did everything she could to keep them up. Elizabeth was a nice looking girl but she was not as developed as most of the girls at her age. At times, she felt as though she was not as developed mentally as the girls her age and sometimes she wanted to be more physically and mentally developed so at times she wondered if she was supposed to do some of the same things. In many cases the other girls were not doing the right things according to Elizabeth's boyfriend.

When it came time for Elizabeth's boyfriend to go off to college, they kind of took things slowly and didn't see each other that much. Of course, Elizabeth was not too bothered about it because she was happy that he was going to college to make something of himself rather than just someone "hanging out" like so many of the other guys. When he finally got off to college, they wrote many letters to each other. Elizabeth received a letter from him one day saying that he had been with another girl in college and to top it all off, she looked like her. Elizabeth's heart was shattered after that letter and began to despise her so-called boyfriend. When she wrote him back, she didn't have any nice things to say. She even sent him a picture of herself, but she wrote some ugly things on the back of it. She was so angry with him that she couldn't write anything nice even if she tried harder.

Elizabeth decided to go on a date with someone else. She thought she really liked this new guy named Eddie, but her cousin told her not to date him because he was found behind the stage with a white girl during drama class. All Elizabeth could do was look in astonishment because she was naïve and couldn't believe that someone she liked actually liked other girls of another race. She never in her wildest dreams pictured this young man with a Caucasian girl, but it was true that most of his friend were Caucasian. Elizabeth couldn't knock it because she had a few Caucasian friends as well. It was sad because Elizabeth went through a period in her life when most of the guys that she liked were hung up on dating only white girls. One of her friends told her that it might be her fate. One day, one of her school mates asked her to go out to dinner with him and his parents. This guy had just broken up with his long time love who happened to be a Caucasian girl. Elizabeth had a wonderful time with this very intelligent young man that loved to play the game called scrabble. He took her to the movies one night and who did they see on the way to the movies, no one but Leroy, her old boyfriend. He looked at them in a strange way, as if she was not supposed to be on a date with anyone else even though he had told her about the girl he was dating in college. She told her date that there was not a problem and to just keep on going. Her date also took her to visit some of his Caucasian friends which happened to be a change change for her. The friend's house was that of a doctor and it was the most beautiful houses she had ever in her life seen. Elizabeth felt privileged to be with this guy but later she began to feel that he still might have feelings for his long time Caucasian love and that he couldn't possibly have any serious feelings for her. She was happy about this because he did not try to get "fresh" with her while they were on any of their dates.

Everybody at Elizabeth's school knew how important high school was even though the guidance counselors didn't help the students too much as far as giving them good sound advice about preparing for college and what would be necessary to complete college. For some reason this information was not given to all students as far as Elizabeth was concerned. Later on, Elizabeth realized how important this information would have been to help her through college. She was given bits and pieces of information from different people but she realized that only the students that had all of the information received scholarships and grants. Nonetheless, most of the students thought about going to college and some of them kind of went with the flow even though they knew that college was very important. Some of the students were just not college material.

Finally, it was time for Elizabeth, the oldest daughter, to graduate from high school and everyone was excited. She was not the only one graduating from high school. Hanna's daughter, Marlene, was graduating also since they were in the same grade and they were the same age. It was a joyous occasion for Dave to see his daughter graduate because even though he only went to eighth grade and didn't finish high school. It was his dream to see all of his children at least graduate from high school. He really believed that graduating from high school was a big accomplishment and the truth of the matter was that for some students it was a big accomplishment. He was so proud when his daughter graduated from high school that he announced that he was going to send her to college and that he wanted her degree to be placed in a special place on the wall above the fire place mantle. Little did he know what the cost would be, he just wanted her to go to college because he had "high expectations" and believed that she could do it. He always gave her words of encouragement and never words of discouragement.

The high school always had their prom for the graduating students. It was a partially split prom though. The black seniors had what was called the "senior dance." Most of them went without dates and it really was a dance and not a prom. They didn't wear the beautiful long gowns or tuxedos at the dance. Basically, the blacks didn't have the kind of money to go to lavish proms with limousines and fancy expensive gowns.

The second daughter, Carla, graduated and he wanted her to do the same thing, but for some reason she did not want to go to college even though one of the teachers came to their house and offered to help get her situated for college as far as scholarships and grants. When it came time for the middle daughter to graduate, Dave had some doubts because he saw how expensive it was and his salary was still very low and the cost of living was going up even higher. The middle daughter was kind of a radical child. Some way she managed to make it all way to the twelfth grade but she was caught up in the freedom lifestyle where the girls didn't wear bras and they smoked just like the boys. The teachers saw this mannerism and reported it many times. So the middle daughter had some problems getting her diploma. Dave and Mary had to come to school many times to straighten out these problems. The boys that she fought with began to laugh and tease her especially when she was walked back up the steps to the office with her parents. She had to attend an adult technical school to finish, but she finished high school and this was the most important part.

Rebecca's peers didn't know what to think and some of them acted the same way that she did. She had many friends which is something she always wanted anyway. Mama Mary said that Rebecca came home one day crying because she thought she didn't have any friends. She fought other students also. She fought one girl one day and they became friends the next day. Anyone could tell that it was an awful fight because they were slinging each other in the mud. Rebecca had many male admirers. Rebecca told her sisters that she had a secret and the secret was that she had been dating a nice young white guy. The idea of Rebecca dating a white guy was preposterous, but she did go on afternoon dates when everybody else was in school. During the seventies interracial dating for black girls was almost unheard of or it was kept in the dark and when you did see a couple like that, it was very shocking as if they had taken another bit of the "forbidden fruit." Interracial dating simply was not accepted by all people yet, even though practically all of the Strong family was mixed with a little Caucasian and Indian.

One day Rebecca came home and told her sister that she went on a date with Jeff to the Golf Course with his dad and that they had a wonderful time. Her sister responded with, "girl don't you know you should try to keep that boy as your boyfriend since you look almost white yourself." Rebecca said, "I will date him for a little while, only it won't be forever because you know he has a girlfriend and she is Caucasian on top of that I don't think that I can deal with that, but I will remain friends with him." "Well I know what you mean as far as that is concerned," said Elizabeth. "As a matter of fact, I couldn't even begin to think of dating a white guy, even though I do get admirers I am not about to let my guard down and be hidden behind closed doors all of the time."

Elizabeth's mind was totally on college at this time. One day out of the blue, she decided that she wanted to go on and go to a four year college. The first year was a little bit difficult because she was working part time as well. At the same time her grandfather became very ill and had to be transported from Tennessee to live with them in Ohio. Again they were faced with the problem of inadequate space in the house. Grandfather George could not help it because he was ill. He had a stroke which left him unable to talk and walk. He lost a whole lot of weight and he could not stand up. He was carried into the house by Dave. It was such a sad sight to see because he was always such a happy and peppy person. You could see in his eyes that he didn't want his children and grandchildren to see him that way but there was not much anyone could do about it. Everybody contributed to nursing him back to health. He would laugh and smile with them every now and then. Dave and Mary had some conflicting thoughts about grandfather being there. Actually Dave was the one that wanted to take care of grandfather even though it wasn't his father; it was Mary's father. Dave had heard from some of his family members that grandfather wasn't being taken care of very well in Tennessee. It was strange that this happened about a year after Dave's father died. Dave had gone to visit Grandfather George in his apartment on a beautiful summer day a couple years before and he seemed to be doing fine but then all of a sudden he was found ill in his apartment.

The job of taking care of Grandfather George became tedious for the girls because they were all doing something, either working or going to school and Mary needed to go to work. Dave, of course couldn't tend to Grandfather George because he definitely had to go to work every day. They really didn't know what they were going to do about this situation. Grandfather did not appear to be making much improvement that year even though it appeared at times that he would seem to be trying to walk with his walker and talk a little bit. He even had a little bell that he rang constantly when he was hungry or wanted to go to the rest room. He loved to ring that little bell. Carla was working at the nursing home, so she learned how to lift him up and how to change his clothing which was a great help. The dreadful thought of taking grandfather to a nursing home was an outrage but with the way things were at the house it seemed that that was the route they were going to end up taking.

Carla decided that she wanted to move into an apartment and make a little room for grandfather so that he wouldn't have to go to the nursing home. Since she was still very young, the friend and landlord needed more information about her in order to approve the lease contract. She didn't have many references because she had never rented an apartment before. She thought, "Oh well, I will just have to tell the friend and landlord that I am going to get married." The friend and landlord believed that she was going to get married because she took a boyfriend with her to see the apartment. Carla really didn't earn enough money to pay for everything and was really not ready for this part of life, so she asked her sister if she would move in with her because it was the only thing she could of at that time. Of course, Elizabeth couldn't just sit and watch her sister move into an apartment without any assistance from her boyfriend. Elizabeth came to the realization that she was going to have to move in with her sister. Everything was going fine for awhile. Everybody that knew them would lend a helping hand with moving furniture and bringing food. Even the friend and landlord helped them a few times. He took them shopping for furniture and other necessities. As they were headed to the shop, they saw Elizabeth's old boyfriend riding a bicycle and he looked them straight in their faces but she again said, "no problem just keep on going."

Later that summer, Elizabeth learned that her high school boyfriend had been using marijuana and that this would probably explain why he boasted of having another girlfriend in college while he was supposed to be Elizabeth's boyfriend. Everybody wondered why he let his fingernails grow so long and why he wore those funny looking wool knit hats all of the time. He just wasn't himself after he left and went off to college. It was said that somebody also stole his car while he was having a good time in New York with some of his marijuana buddies.

He wasn't the only one using marijuana during the seventies which was very unfortunate for many people, especially in this small town. Just about everybody in this small town got what they called "high" because the stuff was running rampant. All they thought about was getting "high" and they knew just where to go to get the "stuff." If he didn't have it somebody else surely did. It was a hindrance to the students' studies and to some of the adults work habits. Even one of Bobbie's so called friends said, "come on over and smoke this marijuana with us." Bobbie replied, "You mean to tell me that you smoke that stuff in your house with your parents there?" Her friend said, "Sure we do because they do it too." Bobbie said, "Wow that is too much for me."

Not only was everybody that knew everybody doing marijuana, the women were taking birth control pills as well as smoking marijuana, drinking and having all kinds of sex. It was just wild and crazy. No wonder they couldn't get their studies and pass their classes. Some of the girls made it through college but they were few and far between. It was a wasted life for many people and studying was the furthest thing from their minds because you could find most of the students in the recreation area most of time. Before most of them knew it, they were dating someone they didn't even like. Along with the equal rights amendment was the freedom of not wearing bras. A lot of girls threw away their bras and went braless. Married couples were having big problems trying to stay married with all of these things going on. The problems were so serious that they wanted to kill one another even though some couples want to do that anyway. While all of this was going on Mama Mary and Dave decided to move grandfather into a nursing home because they simply couldn't take care of him any longer.

They were very sad about moving him there. Mary was so sad that she had to call her preacher brother to come and pray for them and he lived in Chicago.

After a couple of years, to make things even more confusing, Carla decided she would get married to another young man named Gino instead of the guy that she said she was going to marry. Her sister was kind of shocked since it happened so suddenly. It would mean that the two sisters would not need to rent an apartment together anymore. Carla had a simple but beautiful wedding at Mama Mary's house and everybody in the neighborhood was invited. She chose not to have a big wedding because she was already pregnant and she would have felt uncomfortable in an elaborate wedding. This wedding was just right for her. At that time Elizabeth decided to move out of the apartment. Besides, the new couple needed a home of their own. When she moved out neither one of them asked her to stay so that was the end of that, although they did wonder why she left so soon. Things kind of moved smoothly after that because Elizabeth moved right back home because she was not happy with her life at this point anyway. All of Elizabeth's boyfriends knew where she lived and it was dangerous allowing them to butt heads that way. Carla had a beautiful baby girl about six months later. They moved out of the apartment and into a house not far from where they were already living.

Gino's mother visited them quite often. Elizabeth wondered why his mother visited them so often. She soon learned that Gino's mother's husband had been married before and that the previous wife had built a house right across the street from Carla and Elizabeth's apartment. The previous wife didn't care too much for the young group because they loved to have parties at the apartment and she had to go to work early in the mornings. Matter of a fact, the previous wife couldn't stand the sight of the girls having so much company and such a good time. She had two sons by her husband who was now married to Gino's mother and they were very good looking, brilliant and hilarious twins. The twin's mother would not speak to Elizabeth and Carla when she saw them because they were having too many loud parties. When Carla married Gino, the twin's mother kind went into a shell and they didn't see her much. Gino always invited to his mother and stepfather to visit with them at the apartment. Of course, his stepfather didn't have to look very far to see his previous wife who was right across the street.

The twin's were not too happy with the new arrangements in their lives. They tried to make life difficult for their father but they went on to higher education and both of them became pilots and were married. Years went by and everything seemed alright until their father became very ill. Gino's mother was a nurse and took good care of him but for some strange reason he ended up back home with the previous wife and she finished taking care of him until he died. It was rumored that the twins ended up with everything their father possessed and his second wife received absolutely nothing and had to fend for herself. She was blessed enough to be able to take care of herself and she had her own retirement pension so she didn't really need anything that her temporary husband had to offer anyway. Gino was very proud of his mother because she didn't have to ever deal with the confusion that came along with her marriage ever again.

Elizabeth began to date all kinds of guys because everywhere she went somebody wanted to date her and she partied so much that sometimes she didn't get her studies done. She moved back home with her parents and she still couldn't get her life together again. The drugs, the wine and men were invading her life. All of these things together took her completely away from the reality of needing money and intelligence to get an education. She needed some sincere counseling to get back on track.

The newly married couple decided to fix Elizabeth up with a date. She went out on a date with this guy but she could hardly stand him even though they did have a lot of fun probably more fun than she had ever had in her life. Carla and her new husband, Gino still wanted Elizabeth to stay a part of their lives so they introduced her to a friend of Gino's. His name was Fred. Elizabeth had no intentions of becoming serious about this guy but she did party with him. He was really into all kinds of drugs: marijuana, amphetamines, alcohol, barbiturates, nicotine and cocaine if he could get it. Elizabeth didn't realize how deep he was into this kind of lifestyle because he pretended to really like her and he did not appear to be as deep as he was into the drug lifestyle. Because Elizabeth had gained about thirty pounds while in college, she didn't hesitate when they told her that amphetamines would take the weight off quickly. Elizabeth began to take the drugs and couldn't stop using them and the weight came off too. She was down to probably a size four from a size nine at that time. Then along comes another guy to take her away from all of the drugs or either he wanted to join in on the excitement. Elizabeth really couldn't quite tell because of her inability to reason clearly at this point in her life. She was in an unusually bad way. This was quite unlike her because she was always the smart one while in school. For some reason she made a complete change in the way she was living. Her sisters said that it could have been a number of reasons why Elizabeth's life changed so drastically.

Every now and then Elizabeth would be found spending the night with their old friend and landlord who used marijuana religiously. His crib was always dusty from the smoke and ashes even though most of his colleagues thought that his crib was a nice layout. When they got up the next day, they were like zombies which was a predicament that they thought was funny when in fact there was nothing funny about it at all. Really it was plain old ignorance. Mama Mary was furious and she hated the friend and landlord with a passion for allowing this to happen to her daughter. Elizabeth was not allowed to step on his step anymore without Mama Mary behind her. The friction between mother and daughter became even worse than before. From that point on, Mama Mary and Elizabeth would have bitter words for each other. They could barely sit in a room without bickering with each other. Because Mama Mary hated the dope smoking friend and landlord and Elizabeth didn't hate him there was always a conflict. Every time Mama Mary saw him she would become nauseated.

The two guys that Elizabeth dated at the same time were constantly battling over Elizabeth and there were times when they would run into each other when they visited her. She really didn't care if they battled over her because she didn't care for either one of them seriously. The two guys had already had bad feeling for each other because this had happened to them one before in another situation. They fought over another girl named Margaret Ann and she became pregnant by one of them. Both of the guys thought the child was theirs but from the looks of the child it was not Fred's, even though he really wanted the child to be his. It was the strangest thing since most guys at that time were running and hiding trying not to claim children. So because of this particular child, there was a never ending feud between the two of them and Elizabeth found herself in the middle of an awful triangle.

One man was a drug addict and the other man was married. The married man was more persistent and would do anything she asked him to do. She thought to herself many times what a terrible situation she was in. She tried many times to get away from both of them but they kept coming around her. She was still trying hard to go to school and do what her dad wanted her to do. For some reason there were too many obstacles in the way. The whole ordeal began to really get next to her. She had turned twenty-two which was the age at which she was supposed to graduate from college and it was not in the plan for her to graduate at that time. She still needed to do her student teaching and take a few more courses. Still the money was not there nor was the physical energy. She tried to work without a car of her own and go to school at the same time. It was way too stressful for her to even think about. She thought that she would not go to school during the summer and work instead. Elizabeth found a job at a factory office where they made transmissions and was making pretty good money at that, so she moved out into her own apartment.

Everything was fine at first. She was able to get rid of one of her so called boyfriends and that was the one that she could not stand. She even decided to take some classes while working and it was very difficult to concentrate on her work. The job lasted only one year because it was a temporary job but the people that worked at the company made her feel as if it would turn into a permanent position. Unfortunately, several black students ended up working in the factory instead of finishing college. Some of them tried very hard to work and go to school as the same time. Elizabeth worked so much that she became accustomed to the money and being able to pay for everything on her own. When she thought all hope was gone and that she could not take care of herself, the married boyfriend offered to pay for everything until she got another job. He pleaded for her to stay in the apartment. He did not keep his promise to help her pay her bills. She really suffered but she was able and happy to collect unemployment checks. Elizabeth prayed faithfully during this time because she knew that the kind of life she was leading now was just plain sinful.

One day while going to school she saw an old acquaintance from 1972. She had not seen him for years and that was because he had gone off to the Viet Nam War and later reappeared in her life from out of nowhere. He asked her out for a date and she went to dinner with him. It was a very nice evening with no hassles and no worries. The married boyfriend did not know about this activity. Elizabeth wanted this to be her secret because sometimes he was just aggravating and a complete pest, as if he owned her or something even though he was married to someone else.

Mary kind of liked the married man, Daniel, even though he bothered her daughter, Elizabeth. One good point about the married man was that he had great respect for the elderly and he treated all parents with kindness. He didn't hide anything; everything he did was out in the open no matter who saw him or who told his wife. Somewhere along the line he learned how to treat his elders. Mary had mixed feelings about him being involved with her daughter but she tried to guide them as best she could. When the married man's wife found out about her husband's affair, she went ballistic and started telling everybody in the town. She called Elizabeth and threatened to kill her own husband and then she took him to court for a divorce. Later she changed her mind and dropped the case. She went through this same process for years off and on. It got to the point where everybody could see why he wanted to leave her but Elizabeth did not believe in divorce and tried to convince him to stay married to his wife at least for the sake of his children. He did not listen to her and insisted upon seeing her. His wife then threatened to kill them both and then she would say things like "that's alright he has done this same thing before and he always comes back to me. He just wants his cake and he wants to eat it too." He continued to pursue Elizabeth constantly every day.

The married man's wife shot at the both of them one night only she shot into the wrong apartment. The police came and took the wife home. She started acting real crazy so that they wouldn't take her to jail. She told the police that her husband was in there and that she wanted to kill him and the other woman. When Elizabeth and Daniel went out to the car, trash was all over it and gunshots were on the hood of the car. Everybody was a nervous wreck from that incident and Elizabeth wanted so badly to get out of that predicament. He continued to bother her even though he was still trying to work things out with his family. There was something about Elizabeth that he couldn't let go of. Elizabeth began to think that Daniel saw something in her that he needed to help her with but she just couldn't figure out what it was. It was a blessing that Daniel's wife didn't shoot the little boy that was walking around in the apartment that night.

Daniel's wife hated Elizabeth even more now that she had the opportunity to actually get a good shot at them. Elizabeth couldn't shop without her following her from store to store. She couldn't go to school and study like she wanted because she was paranoid about his wife following her and not only that, the married man was following her around also. As if they didn't have anything else to do but follow Elizabeth around the town. It was a complete trip with the luggage for Elizabeth. She couldn't perform well on her job because he would sporadically meet her at work. He was never there when she needed him to be around because he would be somewhere with his wife and kids or some other woman, of course. People around town began to call him a stud and laugh about it at the same time.

Elizabeth decided that before these irrational people got the best of her, she would get out of the picture and date someone else. She went out again with her old friend Eugene and they had another wonderful time. He talked about where he's been since 1972 when she first met him in college. He told her that he had joined the army and that he had even fought in the Viet Nam War. For some reason Elizabeth didn't quite believe him because he took it so lightly, but who knows maybe he did fight in the Viet Nam War. When Elizabeth asked him about the shooting and killing he sort of laughed a little bit but he didn't stay on the subject very long. It was the longest war that the United States had ever taken part in. He began to talk a little bit more about the war. Eugene said that, "in 1957 Viet Cong began to rebel against South Viet Nam's government headed by president Ngo Dinh Diem. So if anyone mentioned that they fought in that war it wasn't taken lightly. March 29, 1973 the last U.S. ground troops left Viet Nam. In 1975, Viet Nam surrendered to North Viet Nam and communist trained South Vietnamese rebels fought to take over South Vietnam. The United States and South Vietnamese army tried to stop them but they did not succeed." Elizabeth began to feel a little queasy about this story then she turned to him and said, "did you have to shoot the guns, did you ever get hurt, are you alright mentally, what else happened?" He smiled at her and realized that this was a very sensitive subject for her and decided to change the subject, but she wanted to hear more about it. He said, "The United States spent 2.5 billion dollars in military equipment to fight the Vietnamese, but even the money that was spent didn't help because France was still defeated and thousands of Americans died, hundreds of thousands wounded and the deceased South Vietnamese exceeded a million. The war left much of Vietnam in ruins and most of the Vietnamese fled the country and some became refugees." Elizabeth said, "Wow that is amazing. I didn't know all of this was going on."

After Elizabeth heard all of this she decided that she would believe him since she didn't see him in 1972, 1973, 1974, or 1975. She didn't see him until the middle of 1976 while in college and coincidentally in the midst of the worst time of her life. They went back to her apartment and watched television and talked for awhile longer. He spent the night with her and they had breakfast the next morning. As they were eating breakfast, there was a knock on the door and lo and behold it was Daniel, the married man. She suddenly got the gut feeling that he may have been watching them because he had done so on many occasions. The only thing she could think to do was to hide Eugene in the closet. It was a very small closet. It was so very uncomfortable for him because it was a very hot day and she didn't have an air conditioner. He was a very tall and muscular man. He was ringing wet with sweat when it was finally time for him to show himself. Daniel entered into the apartment and he sensed that something peculiar was going on. He noticed that breakfast was prepared and this was something that Elizabeth rarely did. She asked him to go and get something from the store for her so that she could get him out of the apartment for a little while. That was a big mistake because his curiosity was aroused even more after that. He searched the apartment and he quickly came to the small closet and found what he was looking for. Elizabeth figured he was already aware of what was going on because he completely refused to leave when she asked him to. What a nightmare, because Daniel was furious and intimidated by this tall, muscular guy. He left the apartment in a rage. Elizabeth thought to herself oh, everything is o.k. now he's gone and she then began to cry. What else could she do, everything was out in the open now. Eugene consoled her and told her that everything would be alright.

It was not over. They heard a loud thump and it was Daniel. The veins were all protruding from of his forehead and his eyes were red as fire. The first thing he did was slap Elizabeth across the face. He then pulled out his magnum gun which was wrapped in a towel and aimed it at the both of their faces. Elizabeth and Eugene were mumbling some words pleading Daniel to put the magnum away. They pleaded with him to calm down. He said, "Ok, I will calm down if you will ask him to leave." Daniel said with his nostrils flared and eyes red as fire, "I'm going to shoot both of you." She looked at Eugene with loving and tearful eyes and then she looked at his muscular body as she softly rubbed his chest. She looked at Daniel and said, "please don't shoot him, please shoot me instead." She asked Eugene to leave and he left. As he walked away, she watched his buff body and thought to herself, "How could I have just completely messed that fine thing up?" If he had shot that gun, both Elizabeth and Eugene would probably have died right on the spot.

Needless to say, her nerves were shot to pieces. She couldn't sleep at night and she had many nightmares about someone breaking into her apartment. One day she told everybody that Jesus came in her room and stood there for a while and started to talk to her. The next night she dreamed that she saw a little girl in her room and the little girl led her to a fire that was downstairs right in front of the building that she lived in. Someone had actually set a truck on fire and left. She was very frightened and decided that it was time to get baptized. She made arrangements to be baptized at her mother's cousin's church in Ohio. She felt that she had done the right thing, but how was she going to get to church every Sunday without a car or some kind of transportation? Obviously, she wouldn't get to fellowship with her church members as often as she wanted to.

It was at this time that Elizabeth's sister Bobbie was about to graduate from high school. She couldn't wait to graduate so that she could get her job and get her own life. When Bobbie went to Tennessee with Papa Dave one summer, Aunt Elma asked her if she wanted to come and live with her. Her house was already crowded, but she liked Bobbie so much that she couldn't help but to ask her to come and live with her. Bobbie went home and thought about it for a little while. She thought since the little town didn't have much to offer, maybe she should go to a bigger city that had better job opportunities. Aunt Hanna bought Bobbie a set of luggage for graduation since she helped her cousin Katherine stay motivated long enough to graduate from high school. Bobbie was happy to get that gift and thought it was simply perfect. So off she went to Memphis, Tennessee. Papa David took her a car so that she could get to and from work, but Bobbie paid for the car herself and took very good care of it.

In the meantime, Albertina's eldest daughter, Michelle, was in Iraq Iran with her husband, so they said. We didn't know if that was really her husband or not since they didn't stay married for very long. Michelle reported to the family that it was awful over there in Iraq Iran. The bombing and fighting continued to go on. They were fighting for oil during the years of 77, 78, and 79. She said that they had to use real hard paper for tissue paper. She simply hated it there.

Hanna's next to the youngest daughter, Marlene, had secretly gotten married and had a beautiful baby boy. Her parents were proud to see their daughter grownup with a family instead of using drugs, alcohol and fighting at the night clubs. But, there were relatives still doing those awful things plus having children. Agnes's sons were heavy into the drug and alcohol scene, using the needle and it was a crucial situation. The eldest son Leonard was so heavy into drugs that he would do anything for the stuff. He bought all kinds of cars to get him to different cities and states. Not only was he using the drugs, but he would sell them as well. Other drug dealers didn't like for him to come around because it was too much competition. Leonard's father hated to see him doing this to his body, just sitting around wasting his life. Even though his father was a stone alcoholic, Agnes still loved him and all of her children and would do whatever she needed to do for all of them. So when Leonard had to go to jail for drugs, she told her husband to sell her mink coat and put a second mortgage on the house to get him out of jail.

Everybody in town knew that he had a reputation of being able to steal all kinds of valuables without leaving a trace of evidence. When he was out of jail, he brought all kinds of stolen clothes to the girls just to see if they would buy them from him. The clothes were so stylish that everybody wanted to buy something, but he wanted way too much money for them. More than anyone had to spare. His brother Richard fell into that same trap except he wasn't quite as bad. He did it mainly because he saw his big brother do it. You could tell that he would do anything to get that "high". People would sometimes see him come out of houses pulling his sleeves down as if he had been "shooting up." It was very hurting for his mom to see this happening, because this was her baby boy. He was so attached to his mother when he was a little toddler that everybody thought he was spoiled rotten. He had to go to jail a couple times also, just like his big brother for one reason or another. His parents had to bail him out even though their money was very low. None of the other family members understood why they kept borrowing money for their boys. They probably figured that it would less embarrassing if they went ahead and paid the bail. They didn't every want to tell their relatives even though it was plain to see what was really happening.

Richard decided he would go to California to live with his sister, Rachel. His sister had spent some time in jail also, only it was because she was hanging with some old gangster type man who was selling everything from the girls to drugs. Anyway she was caught with stolen money on her body and she tried to hide it in an inconspicuous place but it just didn't work. The police found it anyway. Richard went to stay with her thinking that he would work, change his life around and do good like she did. She helped him get a job with computers and he was good for a while but that soon faded out. He was so sprung on drugs that he couldn't kick the habit and he couldn't work. His sister was very frustrated with him and sent him back home where he continued to drink and do drugs. It was a shame because he was a very nice looking young man. Some of the girls went so far to say that he was tall, bright and handsome.

CHAPTER 5:

Growing Into Adulthood

Some of the older family members had gotten together and planned a family reunion. It was finally time for the good old fashioned family reunion. The family hadn't had a reunion in what seemed like decades. The announcements went out to all of the families about the reunion and where it was going to be held. The married man, Daniel that kept coming around Elizabeth was more than happy to go along with them. Everybody was excited about seeing their family members. Not only were they going to see their other family members but they were going to get to see Grandmother Julia at the old schoolhouse. It was a much needed reunion. They ate plenty of good food, went to the nightclubs in the city down on Beale Street and enjoyed the sites. Mama Mary always talked about Beale Street when she was up north. Her daughter Elizabeth always thought she was saying Bill Street and wondered why it was such a big deal according to Mary. Now that she was going to get to visit Beale Street, she would finally get to see exactly what Mama Mary was talking about and was glad to know that it wasn't about collecting money for bills. They had a wonderful time. While they were having a wonderful time Daniel's mother called from Ohio to tell him that his baby girl had swallowed a quarter and had to be rushed to the hospital. Everybody immediately stopped what they were doing and became very concerned about his baby girl. When they took Daniel to the airport to fly back to Ohio, he received another call saying that everything was alright and that he didn't have to rush now. It was like a big bomb fell on the reunion.

A couple of months after the reunion Elizabeth went to the doctor about her nerves that were twitching all over her body which was probably from all of the things that she had been doing. She complained to the doctor that this happened everyday all day. The doctor was not very well known and she was a female. The doctor gave her some pills that she said were for her twitching. Elizabeth thought that this would solve her nervous condition and she felt very confident about this. That night she went out with some old friends. She had such a wonderful time that she stayed out all night. Her sisters were there also and everybody was under the influence of drugs and alcohol and they partied all night and what a mess they were. The guy named Kerry that Elizabeth partied with that night came over to the house and talked with her parents and had a good wholesome family conversation, he even ate dinner with them. He seemed sincere and very nice. It was almost as if the army had changed him into an honest man. But the truth be told, he was not the kind person that they though he had become. He somehow convinced Elizabeth to come with him to the army. With the state of mind that Elizabeth was in, it didn't take much convincing. They took her car and all of her belongings and fled without leaving proper on her job and without a proper good-bye to her mom and dad. Mama Mary pleaded for her not to go. It just broke her heart to see her daughter run off so abruptly. Dave and Mary were just fit to be tired after this incident. Mama Mary would think about what had happened and say, "That Black Mattie left me here." Because now that their daughter was not there and had just about ruined her life running off without the proper necessities.

Daniel, came by one day looking for her and they told him that she had gone to another state. Everybody began to cry. He jumped up and said, "I will go and get her for you Mary." Mama Mary looked up from her sobbing moment and said, "O.K. I would be much obliged if you would." Daniel always volunteered to do things for people. He left and found Elizabeth and tried to get her to go back home with him. He apparently didn't get Elizabeth's drift, because the main reason that she left was because of him and there he was trying to get her to go back home.

Her answer was "no" and to please leave her alone. He became very angry with her again and slapped her across the floor. A big bump appeared on her head from the ring on his finger. He left her there because Kerry called his army friends over and they threatened to hurt him if he didn't leave her alone. Daniel went back home to let Mary know what happened. Mama Mary said, "I did all I could do to bring her back but I couldn't and I am so sorry about that. Thank you, Daniel for trying to bring my daughter back home. It's a shame but it's over now."

Elizabeth stayed with Kerry with very little money and he even spent that up for her. He even got her little retirement check and cashed it. All of her money was depleted and then he took her car. Elizabeth later found out that Kerry was using cocaine all of the time and he played around with other girls. They argued, they fought, he left her alone at night frequently without friends and they were eventually evicted from their tiny duplex. He lied to her so much that she didn't know which way was up. She heard him talking about going to Germany to some of his comrades. Elizabeth saw that everything was happening so fast that she didn't know what to do. Kerry would do strange things and he even acted like the car wouldn't start so she couldn't leave because she had no money, plus she was now afraid that she might be pregnant! This would be a first for Elizabeth and she was very frightened that she would not make it through this episode in her life. He then decided to send her to his sister and his mother in California to live. She flew to California with a few of her belongings after he had thrown away most of her clothes and destroyed most of her shoes. She found some of her clothes in a box in the barracks where most of his friends lived. It appeared as though someone had gone through her clothes for some reason. The whole ordeal began to look so very strange to her. Her poor little luggage fell apart at the airport and some of her belongings were lost along the way. Now she only had a few items of clothing to wear.

While in California she saw more people doing drugs and people hanging out on the streets. She was very afraid and besides she had stuffed herself with birth control pills hoping that she was really not pregnant. Nobody had any money in which to help her get medical attention. She lived from day to day with nickels and dimes from a piggy bank. One day she was looking for a job and this old man tried to talk to her and take her out on a date. She had no idea what would have happened to her, so she dodged every man she could until she finally got away from there. She thought and thought each and every day, "Lord, how can I get away from here?" Kerry told his mother that he planned to marry Elizabeth as soon as he got back and that he wanted to raise a family in California and that she had no money and the only thing she had was a "get away card." The nerve of him to tell his mother about that, she thought to herself. It didn't dawn on her until later that she could actually use that very "get away card" that the university sent to her while she was in college. His sister would say things like, "Kerry is going to come back to California and get us a house to live in." Elizabeth wondered what in the world she meant by "get us a house to live in." Everyday new people entered into the scene and it was so confusing because they claimed to be related and they really weren't.

One day a friend of his sister, Lisa, came by while she was gone to work and sat and talked with Elizabeth for a long time. They had a good little conversation and ate oranges and that was all they did. Kerry's sister swore that Elizabeth was trying to start a relationship with this guy and that she was trying to take him away from her other friend and nothing could have been further from the truth. Elizabeth was already upset with her living situation and she was even more furious now that she had been accused of doing something she had not done. It was so bad that she mustard up enough nerve to call Mama Mary. The conversation was very brief but she could not forget what Mama Mary said. Mama Mary said, "Elizabeth, I had marked you down for dead, girl." Elizabeth didn't know whether to cry or to laugh so she asked to speak to Papa Dave. He was out hunting at the time which is what he normally did every year around New Year's Day. They said their good-byes on the phone. Elizabeth went to her coat pocket and made sure the "get away card" was in place because the first chance she got she was going to "get the hell out of dodge city" one day soon. She got her break, another friend came by, but this guy understood what she was feeling and wanted to help her the best way he could. She asked him to take her to the airport and that is exactly what he did.

She didn't call to make reservations or anything; she just got on the TWA and flew away from California back home to Ohio. It was the longest flight she had ever taken but she was happy to get away from there. She didn't even bother to get all of her belongings. She flew away from there so fast that she left the coat that she kept the card in and it was a nice coat. She really hated that she forgot to get the coat, but she left so hastily.

Grandfather George was still in the nursing home when Elizabeth returned from her disastrous trip to California. While she was there Grandfather George suffered another stroke. Mama Mary was so worried about her father that she called all of her brothers: Adam, Thomas, Paul, Aaron, her sister Ellen and her mother Josephine to come and see about him. Of course, all of them couldn't make it to see Grandfather George but Adam and Paul came down and sang to Grandfather George while he was in the nursing home. He enjoyed it so much that he didn't want them to leave. It was sad for his sons to see him strapped in a chair and rocking back and forth. He had taken a turn for the worse. He could only eat foods like jello and pudding. You could tell that he could not stand living there and wanted very much to just get away from the nursing home, but he was just not able to do that. He never did try to talk again. He just looked at you as if he knew what you were saying and what you were thinking. Mama Mary said that he always did have a photographic memory and he could tell you all kinds of things.

Elizabeth decided that she didn't want to have anything to do with getting married or leaving home for anyone or anybody. She didn't even care about the Viet Nam guy anymore. All she wanted to do was go back to school and get more education, work, travel as she wished and be left alone by any strange characters.

It wasn't easy finding a job in the little town where they lived. As a matter of fact it was almost downright impossible to get a job and keep it. Elizabeth went to the University and was fortunate enough to get a job, but it was a part time position. She enjoyed working part time but she was getting older and the pay was not enough to get her own place or take some courses at the University. Everybody at the University was so nice to her. She didn't have to deal with bosses because most of the people she served were students. Later, she was promoted to a full time position but the boss was very difficult to work with. Elizabeth began to think that the boss who was a female was jealous of her or either wanted something else especially after the way the boss talked to her. One day they had a disagreement over a Comment that Elizabeth made about trying to do better than what she had done. The boss said, "I thought that we had a better working relationship than that." Elizabeth didn't really know how to respond to that statement because no one had ever talked to her in such a manner.

After awhile, some of the same things that happened in the past began to happen. She began to party with her sisters and friends just like before. Many guys wanted to date her even though she didn't want to date anyone. A Puerto Rican college student began to give her the eye every day at work. He didn't know how to approach her especially when the black guys were always around looking at every move she made. A very handsome black guy approached her one day and asked her out for a date. All of the young women in the city knew this guy and wanted to date him at one time or another. He was a strange character but he was more respectable than most of the guys in the town. She thought it was strange though that he was an avid church member but they didn't like him for some reason and ousted him from the church. She decided this guy must need some spiritual help, so she decided that this relationship was not important. It wasn't long before she heard that he was getting married. Elizabeth was shocked to hear this news. Not only did this happen but the Eugene, the Viet Nam soldier was supposed to have gotten married and then another one of her boyfriends got married. Eugene acted as though he wasn't married and tried to keep on dating her, but she was through with confusing relationships such as the married man syndrome.

One night the girls all got together and decided that they would go out and party once more for old time sakes. They were having wonderful time. They saw all of their old friends. It was like a class reunion. The weather was just right, not too hot and not too cold. Everybody had on their shorts and little itty bitty tops. The young men were really out scoping that night. Their eyes gazed upon Elizabeth, Rebecca, Geneva and Wanda. They made their way to Rebecca and set up a date for the rest of the evening. Rebecca went to Elizabeth and told her that this really good looking guy wanted to talk to her. Elizabeth said, "What in the world does he really want and what is really going on?" Rebecca said, "They just want to meet with us for a few drinks." Elizabeth fell for it and went along but she drove her own convertible car to the inn where they all met. The next thing Elizabeth knew was that they were in the inn smoking and drinking. The good looking guy was kissing all over Elizabeth. Elizabeth yelled, "Hold on, wait just a minute, I am not ready for this kind of action." The guy said, "You look so good in those shorts, I can't help myself, I gotta talk to you." Elizabeth pushed him back, but he was very persistent and before anybody could say anything, everybody was wrestling with each other. They were just out of their minds from drinking and smoking and before Elizabeth knew all of the guys were kissing and hugging on her. Elizabeth thought that only the good looking guy was interested in her. Before the evening was over, Rebecca and Geneva left Elizabeth there in the inn with all of those guys, all alone. Then the most horrific thing Elizabeth could ever have imagined happening to her, happened. She was tossed from one guy to then to another, she was horrified and petrified all at the same time. Elizabeth was only able to see a little bit of what was actually happening. When she saw the ugly guy grinning in her face and tossing her around like a rag doll, she came to her senses and realized what was truly happening to her. The thought made her sick to her stomach. After this travesty was over she woke up and saw that all of the guys were knocked out and they could not be awakened. She thought to herself as she slowly tried to rearrange herself back to normal, "GOD must have been with me." She really didn't praise GOD as much as she should have because she really thought that it was she who was tough on her own and that she got herself out of the mess still alive and in one piece. She saw that her convertible was still in order and drove off nervously as she looked back to make sure no one was following her or that no one saw her leave the inn. Later on in life, Elizabeth remembered this incident as a miracle from GOD because she could have died without having time to ask for forgiveness of her sins and could have been on her way to hell that very night.

Then along comes a preacher from Milwaukee who was also a known cocaine user. He was the president of one of the fraternities and he was another married man supposedly going through a divorce. Somehow Elizabeth was always drawn to this kind of drama. Everybody was getting married for some reason but that didn't stop her from going on with her life, even though she had the problem of attracting men that didn't mean her any good. Again, she began to feel that it was her ill fate.

Elizabeth flew to Memphis to see her sister every chance she got which was quite often. She had no thoughts of staying in Memphis since she had already tried to live there not long ago. The same kinds of things were happening as they did every where she went. She thought that things would be different in another town and city, but that was quite the contraire. Plus she was partying at night and trying to go to work the next day. It just didn't work that way. Bobbie said, "Aw come on girl, let's go out to a place called "The Place" and have a good time, it will help you take your mind off of your problems." Elizabeth replied, "Oh girl, I don't need to go out after all of the turmoil I've been through." Bobbie said, "Well, no since in sitting here just thinking about what happened in the past." "You are right sister," said Elizabeth. That very night she met another "no account" guy. They somehow found out that this particular guy smoked all kinds of marijuana and drank constantly like his father and all the rest of the men she dated. Another mess that she didn't need to get herself involved in, A couple of days later one of her relatives wanted to date her. Her cousin immediately told her not to do that because he was related to the family. This was something that simply was not accepted in this family. It was said that if two relative ever had children together, the children would be born with some kind of a serious defect. The thought scared the girls badly. So badly, that the girls decided to go to church with their aunt. The preacher yelled at one of his church members, right in the middle of his message. Elizabeth and Bobbie had never heard a preacher talk to anyone in that tone of voice, so they decided not to go back to that cruel preacher. Aunt Elma loved her church and she was going to stay at her church no matter what they said about the preacher. Aunt Elma loved to fish too but everybody was too busy to go with her or they couldn't get up out of bed in time. Aunt Elma and Bobbie had some nice little talks. One day Aunt Elma told Bobbie that she believed all of Mary and Dave's children would return to Memphis one day to stay. Bobbie said, "Aw I don't know about that Aunt Elma." She then replied with "wait and see." Bobbie didn't do as she said because she was young and not that patient. Aunt Elma was ninety-nine percent correct. All of the children returned to Memphis except for one daughter, Carla. She moved back for a little while but she didn't stay very long.

When Daddy Dave came to Memphis on his yearly visit, Elizabeth got in the car with him and went right back home to Ohio and continued working at the University. Elizabeth and Bobbie continued to communicate with each other although Elizabeth still had no desire at that time to return to Memphis. Bobbie told Rebecca and Elizabeth that she really liked the boy across the street from Aunt Elma and she was serious about this guy. Nobody knew why she was so serious about him, but she was. Before anybody knew anything she had his key and she was living with him in his apartment. He was a nice person and he was very generous with whatever he had to give, but he did not tolerate anything that was intolerable.

Grandfather George became even more ill. One night in February, grandfather had another stoke, only this time his heart failed. He died that night. Mary cried constantly that night and she could barely talk on the phone to her brothers and sisters. All she could say was, "will you all please come to the funeral because I know you all cared about him?" Of course, after the arrangements were made in Ohio, the actual funeral took place at his birthplace in Tennessee. Many people were there and all you could hear was crying and sobbing.

Dave's sister, Hanna had been sick for a long time, too. It was a crippling disease that made her ill. She was happy for so long that everybody thought that she was doing fine but that was not the case. After her second son died, whom they called Bubba, she began to diminish slowly each day. Her second daughter, Louise, was a nurse and she would stay home with her and do whatever she could to help her mother feel more comfortable. It was very difficult for Louise because she had already seen two of her brother's die. She smoked continuously and complained about her nerves all of the time. She was on the verge of a nervous breakdown. Thank goodness she could talk to her cousins who consoled her before that happened. Hanna was very sick and she stayed with them for as long as she could, but one spring day she passed away. The Good Lord called her home. The funeral was very emotional because Hanna's oldest daughter, Lauren, did not take it very well and she cried continuously and before the funeral was over just about everybody in the church had shed a tear or two. She was buried the same day in a beautiful cemetery.

Dave loved his sister Hanna and he suffered through the agony of her death for one year before he became ill himself. One day he was eating some chili on a very cold day and all of a sudden he felt a sharp pain in his chest. It was so unbearable that he quietly told his son Geoffrey to drive him to the hospital. It was determined at that point that Dave had suffered a serious heart attack. He was placed in the intensive care unit for a few weeks. Many people came to visit him but they were not allowed in the room with him. It frightened his girls to see him hooked up to the hospital equipment because he had been strong for so long while living with the bullet lodged so close to his spine. Miraculously he survived the heart attack and he slowly got his strength back, even though there were many things that he could not continue to do. Such as drinking and smoking. Everybody was happy that he was still with them.

Everybody tried to go on with life as usual. Later it was reported that Carla was "with child" for the third time. Again, it wasn't a very easy time for them. Carla was working in the hospital and her husband was still working in the automobile industry and they had frequent lay-offs. Thank God, Dave and Mary kept their old house for them to rent. It was really a blessing even though the house had a few problems plus the fact that it is "hard to go back home once you have left." Their two girls, Teresa and Sara enjoyed living there and when they learned that they were moving to an apartment, they were not very happy. It meant going to a different school. Soon after the baby boy was born, they were packing up to move and the oldest daughter simply threw a fit because she was happy to be close to her grandma, grandpa, aunts and uncle.

Bobbie and Lewis came to visit Carla and her husband after the baby was born. When they arrived in Ohio, little Gino, Jr. had the Chicken Pox, so he didn't look so good but he was still cute even with the little specks on him. They had a wonderful time visiting the family in Ohio. Everybody teased Bobbie and Lewis for living together. They called it "shacking up." They didn't mind being teased because they were happy living together and it was convenient at the time even though they argued a lot about some things. One thing in particular that they argued about was when Lewis called himself going to take a better route to Ohio since it was snowing and the roads were very icy. They ended up going through the mountains in Chattanooga. Bobbie thought, "Oh my God, we are lost!" She was very afraid that he didn't know what he was doing and that they wouldn't make it through the hills and mountains in the snow. Thank goodness they did make it safely. He kept saying everything was going to be alright, but Bobbie kept yelling at him saying, "This is the wrong way!" Somehow along the way he must have proposed to her because they made the announcement later that day that they were going to get married. Everyone was very happy for them so they planned a little party for them while they were visiting. Rebecca said, "I thought they had already jumped the broom when I was down there visiting." Everybody laughed.

The wedding plans were being made. Elizabeth was to be the maid of honor and Pamela was to be the bridesmaid. Their colors were to be lavender and the material was going to be silk and satin. Only special invitations were sent. Of course, the new couple had to select rings for the wedding. They went to the jeweler that they thought had reasonable prices and selected their rings. They were laughing and justa' smiling when they went into the store. The jeweler looked up and immediately recognized Lewis but he didn't know Bobbie. Lewis introduced them. Lewis and Edward graduated from High School together. They didn't communicate too much after High school but they did see each other every now and then. They began to talk and discuss their past, present and the good ole school days. The jeweler, Edward, mentioned that he had gone on to college and graduated and that it wasn't easy. He had also gotten married and had to work to take care of his family. Something had happened to the marriage but he didn't say exactly what except that it ended up in a divorce. Nonetheless, this didn't stop him from dating other women. While they were talking Edward mentioned that he was an ordained minister. Lewis was a member of a Presbyterian Church, but he had not been a devout member and was not quite sure if he should ask the church's minister to perform the ceremony. Edward accepted the invitation to perform the ceremony.

The wedding day was set for October 31, 1982, Halloween evening, which was on the same day as Dave and Mary's wedding. Dave remained calm throughout all of the planning even though it was something that he knew he would have to get ready for. Mama Mary was excited because she sincerely loved being involved in plans such as these.

The big day was fast approaching. Transportation plans were made and everyone would meet up at the church the night before the wedding to rehearse. They got there just in time for the rehearsal. The minister was already there and some of the friends and family. Bobbie's sisters and sister-in-law to be were there. Elizabeth came in with her hair in rollers and a jogging suit looking very nonchalant about the event. The minister saw her bouncing into the church and he couldn't take his eyes off of her particularly her bust. He said a few words to her, but she didn't seem to pay any attention. After all they had just arrived in Memphis after a long drive. She said to her sister, "Why is he looking at me when there are so many women in here that he could look at?" She just wanted to get this over with because weddings made her very nervous and the dresses that they were wearing would make anybody nervous. Because once you put the dress on, you bound to get looked at. The dress had an open v-shaped back and it had a long split on the side. Everybody that saw it said, "Wow!" At the rehearsal the minister whispered in her ear that they would get married to each other after Lewis and Bobbie were married on the same day. It would be kind of like a double wedding only he performed the ceremony. She thought to herself, "What a strange comment for a minister to make." She never thought in her wildest dreams that a minister would say something like that to her. She had so much respect for the clergy and thought that they were a peculiar kind of people. She thought that they should not ever mingle with people who were not quite as religious. She thought that a preacher should always have his bible and should always be at the church studying the word. Although she prayed for other people, she also prayed for herself. She prayed especially when she was in serious trouble or mixed up in some troublesome dilemma and Lord knows she had been in some awful situations. Nonetheless, she must have prayed about this because something was about to happen to her. She did not ponder over his statements, she just said, "I will not worry about that now, because there is always tomorrow." After the rehearsal everybody went home to sit around and talk all night long after they ate dinner. Then they rested for the big event.

The next day while everybody was getting ready for Halloween parties, the family was getting ready for the wedding. Bobbie was worried about getting into her dress. It was not an easy dress to put on and it took all of the girls to help her snap all of the snaps and button all of the buttons because she was very nervous too. Everybody helped her with her hair and her makeup. She looked simply gorgeous as she walked down the aisle. Carla and Gino made it to the wedding. Rebecca made it to the wedding along with them and their three children. Dave was nervous also but he managed to look cool, calm and collected as he walked down the aisle with Bobbie. The wedding was very small but all of the important friends and family were there. The photographer never showed up. Some of the people were happy about that and some of them were very upset. Thank goodness Dave's second cousin was there with his camera. He was able to get a few shots of the wedding for the memory book. Everybody changed their wedding clothes because they were all sweaty from nervousness and they hurried to get into some comfortable clothing.

The people that wanted to go the Blue's Club got in their cars and drove to the night club. They had a wonderful time with a live band and they had drinks galore. Most of them drank a wine called Blue Nun. Everybody got up and danced for a little while and then they just enjoyed the band. The minister even went to the club. This was most surprising to Elizabeth.

After the reception, the newlyweds drove off to their reserved hotel suite down by the Mississippi River. They decided to wait and take a trip to Jamaica later in the winter. They were so involved in their special day that they didn't even notice that the minister and Elizabeth followed them around the city that night. The minister said to Elizabeth, "Wonder what they are doing up there." Elizabeth said, "Probably looking at television knowing them and it is quite alarming to me that you would follow them on their special night. I just don't know what to think of you." The minister began to laugh and said, "Don't even try to figure, I'm just making sure that they are alright." He finally decided to take her home after driving around the city looking at the night scenes. He found it difficult to leave her company though. They kept saying goodnight until Mama Mary hollered out loud, "Elizabeth it is time to get some rest now, you know you have to drive back home." They had the hardest time saying good-bye, but they were both smiling as they exchanged phone numbers and addresses. Of course, both of them had lives already since they were in their late 20's and knocking at age 30's back door. Of course both of them had some fires that had to be put out before they could start a new relationship. They finally said goodnight and parted for the night.

The next day everybody got up from a refreshing night's sleep and had breakfast. Of course, you could not come to Memphis without driving out to the country to Mama Julia's house, the ole school house. It was just the natural thing to do after every event that took place in Memphis. She would stand on her porch waiting for her children and grandchildren to drive up. She always loved the company. If they didn't sit and talk to her for a little while, she would have been very disheartened especially since Grandpa Samuel had passed away.

Elizabeth drove away the next day thinking about her new found friend. Rebecca met a new friend also. Everybody went back to their regular routines. Elizabeth continued dating her friend and she also got a date with one of her own old school mates. Elizabeth never before even gave it a second thought to go out on a date with this guy, but somehow she ended up dating him. Rebecca was dating his brother at the same time and that was probably how they ended up getting together. One night they went to a game together at the college she attended and where she was working at the time. When they started driving along she noticed that he was kind of "lit up," in other words he was "high as a kite." He really should not have been under the influence either because he was still recovering from an accident that almost took him away from this earth. Anyway she tried to keep a smile on her face as they walked up the bleachers. This guy loved basketball and always wanted to play the game. After all of the stumbling and tripping they finally got a seat. She looked around and suddenly got the feeling that people were talking about them and became immediately embarrassed but she finally pulled through it.

When they left the game he got in the car and pulled out this little brown vile filled with "coke" and a little gold spoon and scooped it up into his nose. Elizabeth was so out done. She was so surprised to see him do this thing. This was one of the things that she always ran away from and she wanted to go straight home after that. He wouldn't take her home though. They ended up in another town where she really got sick and ruined the car seat and the side door. He pleaded with her to stay with him, but she couldn't and besides she was thinking about her new found friend. She couldn't understand why anybody with a body such as his, would put "coke" in it. She couldn't tell him any better though because he wasn't about to pay any attention. When she found out that he also had a daughter to take care of, she removed herself from the relationship immediately.

Since she worked at the university young guys were always trying to get her to go here and there around the town but they were really going nowhere fast. Elizabeth began to realize again that the life she was living was not what she wanted but it was the life that she had at that particular time. She began to think that she might as well get used to the idea of living in the same rutty life that she was in and that her life would stay that way for the duration. Elizabeth continued to pray, she continued to study, she continued to date, and she continued to travel. This was the life that she had planned to live and it was the life that many women wanted to live but found it almost impossible with children, husbands and a family life to live.

Elizabeth had dreamed of marriage many, many times. Unfortunately, it was not in the plan when she wanted it to be. Elizabeth talked with her sister, Bobbie, on a regular basis and Lewis teased her about the preacher every time they talked over the phone. At first, Elizabeth and the preacher just talked casually over the phone but then the casual long distance conversations escalated into casual trips to see each other. The casual trips turned into casual discussions, letters and poetry about love and marriage. Elizabeth really could not believe what she was hearing but she wanted to believe it so she began to ask questions. As he spoke of the Bible, she spoke of Sigmund Freud and psychology. She tried to be more philosophical than him but he was an exceptionally intelligent preacher that was knowledgeable in all areas, not just preaching. Elizabeth just couldn't believe it. He somehow turned everything around and made it seem as though she asked him to get married and to have a baby. He joked with her about how it came about but neither one of them really could agree on how the topic of marriage came about but it was finally agreed upon that it must have been in GOD'S plan. Neither one of them were prepared for marriage because both of them lived at home with their parents. It was a small struggle at first but they managed to smooth their finances enough to get started.

Edward came to Ohio to visit Elizabeth one more time to see if she was really sincere about coming to Tennessee to live. Mama Mary seemed to have a very difficult time with Elizabeth leaving her again. She was strong though, she didn't cry. She held her composure and everything was copasetic or so it appeared. The next thing everybody knew, Elizabeth and Edward were loading up the car and one little trunk of clothes. She looked at her parents and thought, surely they won't be lonely after all Rebecca, Carla, Gino, and the grandchildren were still there to keep them company. Dave and Mary were still suffering from the empty nest syndrome even though some of their children were still home to keep them company. It just wasn't the same for them. Rebecca was still working and enjoying her life even though she had been through an awful lot of tribulations in her life already. Carla and Gino were still together even though it was a little rocky every now and then.

Dave and Mary could not get used to the idea that another daughter had left home. They worried about her needlessly and they could not get used to the idea that she was not there with them anymore. She was doing fine. She found a job with an automobile parts company earning a small salary. Since she didn't have many bills, life ran pretty smoothly on her little money.

One day Edward and Elizabeth were sitting on the couch watching T.V. and they decided they would go to the Justice of the Peace and find a judge to marry them. It just happened to be his day off work and she wasn't doing anything that day either. It was almost time for the courthouse to close, but they rushed down with flowers and a camera. The judge was a lady named Nancy Ruzan. She was more than happy to perform the marriage ceremony. Bobbie was there to witness the wedding for them. Afterwards they went to a nice restaurant called "Fridays" for dinner and it was simply delicious. The next day they went back to work as usual. Earning a living was very important, especially during this time in their lives. It was a time when jobs were scarce and the pay was very low. It was hard to provide for both of his children that lived with their mother, let alone their own living expenses. Thank goodness they didn't have car payments to make.

In the meantime, while Dave and Mary was in Ohio taking care of other concerns. Dave's sister's son Leonard had been in and out of drug rehabilitations because the drugs had driven him "off his rocker." He came to their house one day acting really crazy as if he needed a fix or something but he had no money to get anything. So he started "acting out" for attention. Dave and Mary sat him down and fed him some dinner. He seemed to enjoy that for a minute. Soon after that he started throwing things around the house. He would go around and peep into the windows of homes and steal mail out of the mailboxes but if the mail was not someone's check he would tear it up and throw it away. Dave took him to a motel to stay for a little while. It was obvious that he simply was not himself and he didn't care about anyone or where he was. Dave immediately called the hospital and they ended up taking him to a place in Richmond which was where everybody went when they needed mental attention. When he got there, they gave him more drugs such as morphine which made him sick all of the time. He loved to eat sweets which kind of satisfied him a little bit like a kid in a candy store. He was then moved to a closer hospital for treatment. The only thing they could do for Leonard was qualify him for disability.

Leonard's brother, Richard, had turned out to be the same way only he was a little cooler with his problems. Both grown men ended up at home with their mother, Agnes. Agnes had to live with her sister, Albertina in the same house because they had lost their home to the auditors. The house was later demolished. All of them ended up leaving and going to live with Agnes's daughter in Missouri. This worked out just fine for them for a little while.

While all of this was going on up north, Elizabeth and Edward had to move from her sister's apartment to Edward's house with his mother, they finally got their own apartment. The mother of his children didn't take to kindly to him marrying another woman even though she was already in another relationship. Edward saw his children on a regular basis. Family togetherness was very important to Edward, and if he had extra money they would go out to dinner rather than eat at home. He believed that "a family who prayed together stayed together." The children looked forward to those moments. Later they would spend a fun filled day in the park playing basketball, swinging, exercising or swimming in the apartment pool during the summertime.

Elizabeth and Edward decided to go to Ohio to visit Dave and Mary since they hadn't seen them since July. It was now November. They loaded up the car and drove up to see them. They appeared to be doing fine. Papa Dave had made some more wine and he wanted them to sample it for him. He seemed healthy as he walked from one of his houses to the other house. After, the day was over and dinner had been served, Elizabeth decided to take Edward out on the town for the night. They went to the old Highland Café' only the new name of the café was the Talk of the Town. Who would be out that night but the eldest of the two brothers that was in love with Vanessa. They were now married and had two children. Edward instantly noticed that the brother could not stop looking at Elizabeth even though Elizabeth was a conversation going on with Vanessa. Edward could not stand too much of the evening and it was not long before he was ready to leave the party because of the attention that Elizabeth was receiving. So they left the party and went back home. If Edward was jealous, Elizabeth still didn't know it even after they made it home.

Not long after the marriage and after they moved into their own apartment, they discovered that a new baby was on the way. All of her family and friends were excited about this because here she was about thirty years old and having her first child. Elizabeth didn't quite know what to expect. She was sick every morning and thought she could handle the sickness but it was unbearable. The doctor gave her some medicine which helped a bit, but the sickness did not go away completely. Her mother told her to wait after three months and the sickness would subside. Elizabeth said, "Oh, do I have to wait that long?" Edward's mother was very helpful with cleaning and cooking for them. She was that kind of a person, she loved everybody and it didn't matter who it was even if it was the junky on the street. As the days went by, she began to get bigger and bigger and it was perfectly normal. Only she had to have the shots because of her blood type. In the old days, people with her blood type were not encouraged to have children. Most people didn't know what their blood type was, so they had children anyway. Some of the children were born with deformities if the other parent had the wrong blood type. She was so thankful to the Lord and the new medicine for giving her a healthy baby. It seemed that no one knew how thankful and how happy she was, so she tried to adjust her feelings to make it seem as though she was normal and that this was nothing that was so spectacular. Deep down inside she knew that this was a miracle, a blessing and that the Lord was with her the whole time. As she enjoyed her moments with her new baby, everybody resumed their normal activities. Edward continued to visit his children and bring them over to be with their new baby sister. Elizabeth felt as though she was more involved with his x-wife's family than her own family. She heard his x-wife's name more than she heard her own sister's name during that period in her life. It was so depressing for Elizabeth to have to hear all about her husband's x-wife's family conditions during that time frame.

As the family was enjoying their lives and Edward was aspiring to be a preacher, rumors were brewing in the church. Elizabeth was not used to attending church regularly, but since she was married to an "ordained preacher" it was only natural for her to attend and be by his side at all times. A lot of people would say that that was the right thing to do. It was different from anything she had ever done in her whole life. She learned that all preacher's wives have to go where their husband's go and that it was mandatory. She learned that other men and women were always watching them, the way the wife dressed and the way she acted. It was definitely a change for her. Edward's previous wife would even come by the church occasionally to be on the scene. It was rumored that she was not happy with Edward being married again and that some of her friends could have been from the same church. They encouraged her to take him to court for more money.

Edward would get all kinds of calls anytime of the day for something or the other. They began to call if they needed a bag of candy for school, if they needed a pair of tennis shoes, if they needed a way to school, if they needed a car, if they needed medicine, if there was no food in their house, if their teacher yelled at them and many more emergencies. It was enough to have Elizabeth singing the blues. The children were basically good and they honored both of their parents. Some of the people would tell the current wife, Elizabeth, what was going on and his previous wife would always say that it was just for the children and that he was to take care of his children or else. Elizabeth and Edward did all they could for the children. He even worked thirteen and fourteen hours a day just to make enough to take care of them. Sometimes when they took the children out for the weekend and brought them back home, the previous would not be there and they had to find some place to take the children so that their mother could pick them up. Usually, it was after 12:00 midnight when they found a place for them to wait for their mother. This really did not sit well with Elizabeth because she was concerned about the children getting their proper rest for school the next day and she needed her rest also since she was with child.

Strangely enough, when the children grew up to college age it was still rumored that she was still trying to keep a ruckus going on with Edward and Elizabeth. It may not have been true, but it seemed like she would have done any and everything to see his new marriage fail. Both families said that that was a hush! hush! thang. She used all kinds of stumbling blocks for Edward to make life as miserable as possible for them. Every man she met, she found something wrong with him so that she could be free of a husband. Elizabeth was alarmed at how this woman carried on but then she remembered that she had been through something similar to this a few years back. She remembered having an argument with one of her high school boyfriends about how history repeats itself. She remembered telling him that it was not a true line. But it seemed that the previous wife would focus on irritating her previous husband and his wife. She made it clear to all of the good people in her life that she didn't want any help from them because she really didn't want to be bothered with anyone. She just wanted to make hell for Elizabeth and Edward and then act as though she had done or said nothing wrong. Everything he did, she had to get her two cents in one way or the other. Someone told another person that they heard that she even called the new wife up and cursed her out calling her all kinds of witches, bitches, whores, and adulteresses. That woman called her everything but a "child of God." No one knew how true it was, but it was a rumor around the town at that time that she called her all of those ugly names. That became another one of those, "hush, hush thangs". Elizabeth was upset but again she remembered that she had already been through something very similar to this kind of problem. She remembered how she was almost shot by Daniel's wife and how he almost shot her as well. Elizabeth could really say, "been there, done that." People would whisper things saying that the previous wife would do anything to discredit the current wife and would say anything to make her feel like she was nothing. People around town would gossip all of the time saying that the previous wife took him to court several times for more money, anything devious to make life miserable for the new couple. No one knew how true that was either but it was whispered around town.

Elizabeth's sister Bobbie was always comforting when Elizabeth was having difficulty understanding if she could deal with her marital situation. Bobbie suggested that they all go out to the Club Honolulu. Elizabeth, Edward, Bobbie and Lewis went out and had a good time. Elizabeth began to feel a little wheezy and her body felt limp as they were leaving the club. She called out for Edward to catch her as she started to fall. The owner of the club said something ugly about Elizabeth. He said, "Oh, she is just on those drugs." Bobbie said, "She is not on drugs and if you say that again, we are going to shoot you with this pistol." The pistol was Elizabeth's shoe which had a heel on it that was about four and one half inches. She pointed the heel towards the owners face. They never went back to that club again. Later, it was all over the newspapers that the club had burned down to the ground. Elizabeth was in shock and wondered what happened to the club. Lewis began to tease her and say that she made that happen.

Elizabeth jumped up and said, "That is totally not true and I wish you would never say that again in your life."

Later that month, a hearing was set for Edward and his previous wife, Lula. The current wife visited the courtroom that day and before the hearing started everybody was kind of just wondering around the building. Some went to the restroom and some stayed in the courtroom. It just so happened that the previous wife, Lula and the new wife Elizabeth were in the restroom at the same time. Neither one said anything to the other one because of the obvious reason why they were there; they just gave each other some very strange looks. It looks could kill; they would have killed one another. One of the persons in the courtroom said that Lula looked Elizabeth up and down and then frowned and turned away. Someone else in the courtroom said that Lula tried to make the judge take part of the current wife's little paycheck and all at the same time there was gossip around town that Lula was having fun partying at all of the juke joints picking up all kinds of men. No one really knows how true that was but it was one of those hush! Hush! thangs. Some of the town's people said that the current wife was really agonizing over how a woman with a man's children could make him feel so down trodden and guilt ridden especially when she knew that he would do anything for his children.

The current wife Elizabeth was all in the middle of this uncomfortable situation never knowing who was talking about her and whether they were saying that she was a mean old stepmother or what. All she could do was call on her mother, her grandmother, her other grandmother and her sisters. They all tried to console their sister, but it was still very difficult to be at ease in the marriage. She never knew what craziness she would face from day to day. Still she held on. Grandma Josephine said, "Gurl don't you worry about that crazy stuff, just pray day and night and read your bible and remain in the Lord." Grandma Julia never said much, she just gave her a loving smile every time she saw her and said, "Come on in the house child." Grandma Julia had gotten a little older now, but she could still talk to you on the phone sometimes. Elizabeth talked to her sister Bobbie and brother-in-law all of the time. He always tried to cheer her up with his spirits. Her mother would tell her to keep on going as any independent person would do. Then she told her not to let those kinds of things worry her. Her mother, Mary always wanted her children to be as independent as possible because she had witnessed so many problem marriages as well as her mother's marriage and her own marriage. At the same time divorce was not an option. Elizabeth got through those days by the grace of God. Thank goodness Edward was a God fearing young Christian or else they probably would not have gotten through their marriage let alone worrying about the other problems that came their way during that time. Edward would go to Grandma Julia's house with her sometimes, but not enough according to the family. They didn't get to know him quite as well as they knew Bobbie's husband. Lewis was there quite often fishing or just enjoying the open fields. Grandma Julia and Uncle Timothy knew him quite well.

Edward didn't go there very much because he was either at work or somewhere picking up his children, as his previous wife would make sure he did or else she would raise all kinds of holy hell. If he didn't, she would just send him on another guilt trip. She was well known for doing that and she was also well known to just kill any kind of joy either of them might have made for themselves. Come to find out she had gotten rid of her main boyfriend, the one that was taking care of her. She was secretly dating another man. Everybody in her neighborhood was talking about her and wondering what in the world was wrong with her dating all of those men around her children.

Elizabeth tried to cook to ease her mind from all of the drama. Elizabeth prepared a dinner for Lewis and Bobbie because she wanted to entertain company to do something other than thinking about her marriage constantly. One of Elizabeth's co-workers had given her a carrot cake recipe to make from scratch. Elizabeth made the cake, but for some reason it didn't taste like a carrot cake. Everyone talked about Elizabeth's carrot cake, even Elizabeth talked about her own cake. They enjoyed the evening and many days after because Lewis continued to tease her about the cake and the evening at Club Honolulu. It was always a good laugh because Elizabeth really thought the carrot cake was going to taste good.

CHAPTER 6:

Back On The Home Front

Elizabeth didn't dwell on the fact that Edward didn't have ample time to be with her every time she went to her relatives' house because it would only make her sad to think about it. She had been through enough turmoil to even begin to let that bother her. Elizabeth focused mostly on her immediate family. She had heard many, many times that "blood is thicker than water." Elizabeth heard that Albertina's daughter Katrina was diagnosed with a very bad illness. Then one day Elizabeth remembered what her aunt Agnes said, "Time waits for no one." The family didn't know if it was cancer or something else but the doctor's said that she was very ill and that she was in serious pain. She hollered all night and all day because of the pain. The doctors did everything they could for her but nothing seemed to help. It was finally decided by the doctors that she would not pull through this illness. The family was very sad to hear this news especially since she was so very young, approximately thirty-six years old. All of her cousins wanted to come and see her but it was too late. She passed away and then there was no more pain and no more crying. Her funeral was so quick that very few members were able to attend the funeral, especially since it was so far away. So the family talked about it for a little while and went on about their business working going to school or whatever.

One day Elizabeth and Edward were just sitting at home, when all of a sudden they received a call from Mary. Dave had left Ohio and was on his way to Memphis. He was traveling alone. He didn't look as well as he usually did. There seemed to be something wrong with him. Dave visited with all of his family members and carried on as if everything was fine. He enjoyed several days at the house with his mother but for some reason he wanted to get his own apartment. He was having some problems with his sisters and brothers about building a house on the undivided property that was owned by all of them since their father did not divide it for them.

Grandpa Samuel knew that if he did divide it, they would still have problems with who was going to be located where on the property. While Dave was trying to make plans to build a house he became ill and had to go to the hospital. It started with a little knot on his back that would not go away. When he went to the hospital they told him that he would have to stay for a little while. Lewis and Bobbie called Mama Mary to tell her the bad news. She said, "I told him that he did not need to go to Memphis especially since he had already had one heart attack and had been placed in Intensive Care at the hospital in Ohio." She was really frightened about his health. Mary took the first flight to Memphis. She had not flown very much but she seemed to handle it pretty well. Everybody went out to the hospital to see David and the doctor was already waiting on the family to tell them that he had suffered another heart attack and that his chances of making it were very slim. David had many other complications. The family was afraid and very sad to hear this news. Mary decided she would just stay at the hospital for the night until they could tell her more detailed information. She was told that they would have to do surgery and he would have to stay in the hospital for a good while. Miraculously he came through the surgery just fine and he was able to resume his normal activities. He went deer hunting, fishing and rabbit hunting as he usually did. When the family asked why he was out doing all of these things they were told that the doctor wanted him to be active rather than just sitting around moping. He had to go back to the hospital for testing regularly. He loved the treadmill because it made him feel alive as though he was actually going somewhere and he loved to walk. He had to watch his diet very closely and that was very difficult for him because he liked everything from pickled pig's feet to barbecued ribs plus he would drink a beer every now and then. The doctor said he could have a glass of wine to help build his blood every now and then and that made him feel better to know that. Before he had gotten sick again he tried his hand at making his own wine. Dave was like that and he loved making his own things and he always shared with everyone. Whenever he cooked, he always asked whoever was around if they would like to have some and it was always fingerlinkin good, especially his barbecued ribs. If he had some vegetables in his garden he would pick them, cook them and if anybody in the neighborhood wanted to get something from the garden they were more than welcome.

One day everybody was just sitting outside talking and Bobbie observed a different lump on Dave's back. He went into the hospital for the lump on his back. The doctor did some research on it and they discovered that it was cancerous. This was devastating news to the family because they had just recently gotten over the horrendous news about Albertina's daughter and the heart attack that Dave had had just a few years before. Everybody thought that he would not recover from that because when the doctor told the family it was hardly likely that he would make it. The doctor said that there was not much left of his heart and that the family would have to be very careful with him. Well, the family just went to pieces because they depended on Dave for everything from advice to fixing things for them. He was known to many people as a genius in the area of fixing everything from houses to cars. No matter what happened to him he always felt that he could bounce back and overcome his problems. But, when the doctors told him what was going on with his body, he began to fall in a slump and was not quite sure how he would conquer this one problem. Many of his family members had died from this cancer and he remembered how his father died from cancer. He cried, prayed and walked a whole lot but the disease was there and it was not going to leave because it was malignant and it had already spread throughout many parts of his body. He never poured his problems out on his children because he always wanted them to be happy and proud of their father. He didn't have the need to talk much about his illness because his children loved him dearly and they could see that he was not at his best but they stood by him nevertheless.

Since time was not waiting on anyone, Dave decided that it was time to confess his belief in Jesus and get baptized. The announcement was made to the family that he and Joseph would be baptized on the same day. The family made ready for the special day and would not have missed it for anything in the world. The day finally came and it was a beautiful sight to behold when they were baptized in the old pool outside of the church, just like in the olden days. People were all around the pool taking pictures and praising the Lord and Savior at the same time. A smile came over Dave and Joseph's faces after the ceremony was over. It was a smile of relief just to know that they were able to be baptized and repent at this late time in their lives. Everyone prayed that the Lord would hear their pleas and accept them on judgment day, into his kingdom. After the ceremony, dinner was served and once again they shared a lovely day. Bobbie & Elizabeth had gone to get their hair done the day before that and Bobbie's husband had just bought a car. Bobbie was flying down the street in her car and the police stopped her. He proceeded to get out of the police car and walk towards her car. He began to ask questions like, why was driving so fast and did she have a driver's license? All she could think of was her father. She told him she was in a hurry because her sixty-two year old father who was a cancer patient was getting baptized that day. He still gave her the ticket though. She thought to herself what a mean old policeman.

No matter how hard the times got, no matter if they didn't have a penny to their names, they were still proud to be his children. The doctors gave him radiation treatments for cancer. The first treatments made him lose his appetite which was really unlike him. He always had a strong appetite before the treatments. He lost quite a bit of weight and his energy level was not the same. Mary said that he had gone into "remission" when the children asked about him. They called to ask about him all of the time. Dave's children were very happy to hear that he was up and about, hunting as he usually did. But when he was in bed and not feeling like getting up the children were not happy. He lost all of his beautiful hair and became bald. He laughed about it for a while and called himself "Kojack" and that made everybody laugh right along with him. He listened to music on the radio and his children thought he never listened to music on the radio especially the same music that his children listened to. It was almost as if he was trying to tell them something but couldn't bring himself to break their hearts so he just played music and pulled his hair out as if nothing was happening to him.

There was a problem when Dave decided that he wanted to build a little house on the property. Nobody would sign the papers for him to build because they couldn't see why he would jeopardize his health even more by building a house. They were very skeptical about the whole idea of it since he was sick and on chemotherapy, but he was bound and determined to build something on the vacant property that had been in the family close to one hundred years. Sometimes he would cry when they told him he shouldn't chance building the house. He finally obtained a permit to build it but it was not totally his house even though he built it. The property was still not divided and deeded to anyone in particular. He went on hunting as if he was not sick because his doctor told him to try to stay active or he would stop altogether. He ate very light foods such as, oatmeal for breakfast, boiled and baked chicken or fish for dinner. None of his food was cooked in hot oil because boiled and baked foods helped his digestive system tremendously. His diet was important because besides the cancer he also had a serious ulcer. The ulcer did not stop him from working on the house. His brothers came down in the spring to help him work on it.

He was outside working on the fence one day and Matthew came by to see him. They sat for a minute and he had a heart to heart talk with Matthew. He said to Matthew, "I am not going to live much longer, but I don't want anybody to take what belongs to us. Don't let them take our history away and be aware because they certainly are going to try. I tell ya, they are gonna try. You never know what your peoples will do to ya, man, you just don't know your own peoples. We have had this land since 1900 so why do you think anybody would want to let someone else come and take what our grandfather works so hard for? Why in the world, just why, why?" Matthew said, "I don't know Uncle Dave." "Well you do what you can to help them keep it son." Dave didn't talk to his daughters about the property because he didn't want to burden them with it.

Daddy Dave and his grandson taking a ride
around the property on one of the days that
he was feeling better in 1987.

He did everything he could to make life easy for his children but
it didn't work because the girls felt the burden anyway because they
could see he was sick especially when he was in the hospital. He began
to look weaker and weaker. The medicine made him appear to look
like he was looking off into another whole direction. Elizabeth asked
him if he would have liked to see some other places or is this where he
wanted to be? Dave quickly answered with, "I only want to be here,
no other place." Again the family came to see him in the hospital and
miraculously he pulled through his stay in the hospital once again. He
immediately went back to work on his house again. He was so happy
when he put the pipes in the house for running water throughout the
house. He was so proud of himself. It got to the point that he could
barely stand up to stir the wood in his pot bellied stove. It was the late
1980's and he wanted a pot bellied stove even though he was used to
all of the modern heating systems. Thank goodness someone was there
to stir the fire up for him or he probably would have fallen to the floor.
He did not get mad at anyone like many people did when they were ill.

He just went back to the sofa and sat down with a smile on his face. He then took his cane and pointed at the stove and told someone else to go and stir it up. His skin was very dry from the medicine. They oiled him and oiled him but his skin was still very dry.

Dave was having a difficult time going to the bathroom by himself. He still wanted to be too proud to tell anyone about his illness but he finally humbled himself so that his daughters could help him to the car when he went to the hospital. One night he was in the hospital and Elizabeth came to see him and do whatever she could her him. They talked for a long while, until he went to sleep. Elizabeth stayed there watching television for awhile. She looked at him and became frightened because he was in a really deep sleep. His arm plopped down on the side of the bed and she thought he was gone at that moment. She checked to make sure he was okay and decided she would go home and get some rest for herself. It was hard for all of his children to accept what was happening at this time.

The girls and Mary alternated going to see after their father while he was in the hospital and took the special foods that he could eat. While Daddy Dave was in the hospital, everybody did and said everything they could to make him laugh and stay awake. One day Lewis was in the hospital with them and he started making up stuff to say. All of a sudden he started talking about the Club Honolulu. He told Daddy Dave all about the night when Elizabeth was intoxicated, almost passed out and tried to shoot the owner with her shoe. Daddy Dave looked around and said, "What? She tried to shoot the man with her shoe?" Then everybody began to laugh. Lewis started to laugh so hard that he couldn't tell the part about how the building somehow burned down to the ground. Daddy Dave laughed softly, but it was a hearty laugh considering his condition. Geoffrey spent a lot of time with Dave. He helped feed and bath him every day and it was really something for him to experience.

Miraculously, Dave was able to go home even after that night. He told everybody that everything was going to be alright and that he was going to get all of his muscles back as soon as he gets well. He did get strong enough to drive a standard shift automobile and amazingly he was strong enough to do little odds and ends work on the house. Even though he was sick he seemed to be at peace with himself. He had no worries at that point and time in his life. For one thing, he was happy that he was a born again Christian at such a late time in his life. He didn't know he could be as happy and blessed as he had become even though his family was falling apart. He did all he could to keep the family together and everybody loved him for that. Papa Samuel had left Dave in charge of everything when he died because he knew that Dave loved and respected everything that his forefathers had worked for.

It was getting late in the year of 1988 and his house was not finished yet but as far as he was concerned they could live in it. Elizabeth asked, "Dad don't you want to live in one of those huge houses?" He answered with, "No, I do not want a huge house because the utilities would wear me out?" It still needed some painting, kitchen cabinets, and a shower stall but he chose to stay there anyway even though he was terminally ill. The weather started to change quickly and so did Dave's health. One day he had the desire to go Christmas shopping since it was getting close to that time anyway. Even though he could barely walk like he used to, he still wanted to go to Wal Mart and look around at the Christmas goodies. He loved shopping for others around Christmas because his birthday was on Christmas day and this made him feel better. Dave even named one of his horses Christmas. Dave's children and wife could see that he was having a very hard time trying to shop so he had to have a seat along the side because he did not want to fall down in front of his children. He was too proud to do that. He looked up at his family and smiled at them and asked, "Would you all like a candy bar?" All the girls could do was look at him and say, "Thank you daddy, yes, we want a candy bar." It was the epitome of the simplest goodness anyone could have ever thought of. He was able to get up and walk after that and they all went home to the little house that he built. The house was so close to Grandma Julia that it was really like going home to Grandma's house.

Dave went home and got some well deserved rest. He told them that he also had a box of chocolates in the trunk of the car, but he couldn't give it to them because he had to hide it from Mama Mary because she might eat them all up. That was just a little joke between them because she really didn't mind eating and that was why she had become overweight. After the shopping was all done Dave was able to enjoy his Christmas even though he was bed bound. He just felt good to have been able to be a part of the Christmas shopping festivities. He was even able to eat turkey, dressing, pumpkin pie and turnip greens just like he did when he was a young lad and living with his Ma and Pa. He continued to raise his livestock even though they got hungry and tried to wonder off the land. He somehow managed to get them back where they belonged especially after the neighbor complained about the hogs getting in his yard. He was a very nice neighbor he just didn't want the hogs in his yard eating everything in sight. Dave often wondered why Papa Samuel sold that particular area to the neighbor and then left some land on the other side of the neighbor. It was a mystery that he could never figure out. But now that his health was seriously failing he didn't worry about too much of anything.

Dave loved to celebrate New Years' day and it was fast approaching. New Years' day came and Dave listened for the guns to start shooting. This was always an exciting time of the year for them because they loved to go to parties. This year was not going to be one of those years, so he stayed home and watched the excitement on television.

Dave and Mary prayed each day and night about the pain that he was feeling. The pain was so excruciating that he had to continuously make visits to the hospital. The doctors decided that he needed more blood because of his red and white blood cells, not to mention what the chemotherapy had already done to his body. The doctor would get him well enough to go home for a few days and then he would have to return to the hospital for a few more days. This process continued for months. The pain grew more and more excruciating until finally he was hospitalized again, only this time it was for more blood. The morphine was discontinued. The blood would stay in his body only for a little while and then it would just come right back out of his body. His body just would not hold the blood, especially with the ruptured ulcer in his intestines and the weakened veins from the radiation. The chemotherapy and medication was too strong for his already weak body. The nurses continually cleaned his bedpan and changed his bed clothes. The nurses and orderlies were running around to get more blood for him but the ulcer had burst and it could be mended. He bled continuously. Everything that came out of his body appeared to be blood and water. It was frightening to see this thing happening to Dave especially for his daughters and son. He was already as thin as anyone could get with a 6'4" frame. The smell was so strong that even the nurses and orderlies could not stand it. They ran and hid for several minutes. They used lots of Lysol to cut down the odor. It was like someone hanging from a tree and no one could reach him and bring him down. Somehow through all of this turmoil Dave's body was stabilized again.

That one day he lay there looking peaceful as if he was going to be just fine for at least another year. When he woke up he was talking and everything as if he knew what was going on around him. He even talked about a little business and said his children's names. Everybody felt comfortable for a day as if he was going to pull through this and come home with them again. He stayed in the hospital for another day. Carla and Rebecca slept at the hospital and visited with him the next morning. Everybody else went home to get ready for another day. Carla put her arms around him as she prayed with him and he said, "More mercy, more mercy father!" He thanked the doctor for all that he had done for him. At 11:30 a.m. on December 10, 1990, he left the hospital and his family. He laid there cold as ice and his mouth was all the way open as if he was taking his last breath or maybe he wanted to say one more thing. Mama Mary could hardly move herself from the chair because her body was numb. She just looked at him and said, "Will someone go over and try to close his mouth for him, please?" Everybody turned around and looked at her as if to say, "What is she thinking about and where did that come from?" Elizabeth tried to do what she asked, but it did not work. They came to the realization that Mary was in a state of shock as was the rest of the family. This was the man that she depended on for everything and he provided all that he could for her and the children for at least thirty-six years. She just couldn't stand for him to leave so soon.

Suddenly the room was quiet as if he was just lying there sleeping as he usually did when he was tired and wanted to rest. Then Elizabeth's husband reminded her of what Papa Dave said a few months before he died. "Yes, I remember that he said he was going to get his muscles back," sobbed Elizabeth. Elizabeth began to cry profusely because he didn't get to do that before he died. Then she said, "Oh well, I will see him again in heaven with all of his muscles." Everyone left the hospital to make ready for his funeral. It was not a very easy thing for the family to do but thank God for the loving and caring family and friends. Of course Dave had many, many friends. Flowers and cards came from everywhere. The small church where he accepted Christ as his savior about one year before he died was filled with people. It was not so important to have many people give speeches at his funeral because it was so apparent that he was liked and loved by so many people. No one said a negative word about the simple arrangement of his funeral. Usually people made remarks about what they thought should have been done and what they wouldn't have done, but nothing was talked about. The preacher mentioned that it was a good thing to accept Jesus Christ in your live even at age sixty-five. As the preacher was giving the eulogy, he began to talk about the storms that come and troubles that come and he began to get very excited about what he was saying then suddenly he started turning around and around as if the storm was right there in the pulpit. You could tell that this particular funeral touched his heart deeply. The people met with each other and tried to console each other after the funeral, they followed the Hurst to the cemetery where Dave was buried.

For days, weeks, months and years the family thought about Dave and how much they missed him. All of his daughters declared that they had received visits from him and that they talked to him at night. One thing that stood out in all of their vision of Papa Dave was the shoes that he used to work in or the white horse that he rode and the white clothes that he wore. They all agreed that he was truly showing up in their lives. Sometimes it was frightening and other times it was comforting to them. Either way, he was welcomed by all of his children and Mary, his wife. It was something very new in their lives and it was going to take a long while for them to get over the death of their father. The concern now was to get on with their lives if at all possible.

It certainly was not easy to go on because about one month later David's eldest brother passed away. They were always very close brothers. They went hunting together, played cards together, worked on houses together and traveled together. Whenever David traveled to see their Mama Julia, Joseph went with him. They loved going to the old schoolhouse and they wouldn't want to change it for the world. Everyone remembered the day that Dave and Joseph were baptized. It was so meaningful to see them be dipped in the outside pool the same way it was done many, many years ago. In their last days together, they put up a new fence around the estate even though both of them were very ill and they went to church together.

Joseph's funeral was held at the same church and he was buried in the same cemetery. Soon after Joseph was buried, Agnes' son, Leonard died accidentally in his brand-new corvette. Lillie's son Tyrone died a few months after that. Both of their birthdays were on the same day as Dave's. People were saying that death comes in threes. It was a classic case of three consecutive deaths in the immediate family.

Mama Julia was very sad about all of this and began to get weaker and weaker as she aged. She was now at the age of ninety-five and now two more of her own children had succeeded her in death. So naturally, the whole family was very concerned about her. Sometimes they were overly concerned to the point that it bothered her and her other son, Timothy. They thought in their minds that they were getting along just fine in spite of it all, but there were some things that they needed help with, like going to the store, to the doctor and making sure their laundry was done. Everybody kept talking about them. They were saying such things like they were not being taken care of like they should. Of course, this was a "hush, hush thang" among the family and neighbors. When the immediate family found out about it, they were embarrassed. This forced them to feel a little bit of guilt. One of her children, Albertina felt that since she had retired from her job and was not working anywhere at the time that she should move her belongings to Tennessee from Ohio even though she had two houses that needed her attention. She dropped everything right then to take care of her mother. Lillie also felt the same way and decided to stay with Mama Julia for a little while also, but she didn't drop everything to take care of her mother. The two sisters were in their seventies themselves and they were not in the best of health. Their children were concerned about them also and wondered if they would be able to handle taking care of Mama Julia. The two sisters told the neighbors and relatives that their mother was not able to take care of herself and that they wanted to move her away from the schoolhouse that everybody visited when they came to Tennessee. They wanted to move her in a house with them even though they didn't have a house or an apartment in Tennessee at that time. Most everybody thought it was good that someone would be looking after Mama Julia but they just couldn't imagine her not living at the old schoolhouse. As a matter of fact, her close family, the neighbors and all the people who went to that old schoolhouse thought that she should continue to live right there and let a relative move in with her. All of Joseph's children hated to see Mama Julia be taken away from her home. The grandchildren cried, "Please don't take Grannie away from here."

Mama Julia's son Timothy didn't want them to change anything either. He felt as if everything was fine the way it was and the two sisters were invading their home. The two sisters still felt that Mama Julia needed to be watched, daily. Timothy was very angry about these changes and decisions and the fact that he had lived there all of thirty-five years and had gone to school there for ten years. This was not going to be easy for him to accept. One day he was so upset with his sisters that he stormed out onto the porch and fell off one of the steps which left him paralyzed. The two sisters took him to the hospital where Albertina's daughter worked and it was there that they took care of him. He was not in a coma, but he was not able to move about. All he could do was look up at the ceiling. He would smile and nod his head as if he understood everything that was being said.

The nurses all loved him because he was such a nice patient. The doctors and nurses told family members that he probably wouldn't make it and if he did he would have to be confined for the rest of his life. The cost to do this would be phenomenal. The cost would be way beyond the amount that anyone in the family could afford and his only child was killed many years ago so he had no children or wife to care for him consistently. The family still prayed for him and prayed that he would be alright and that something miraculous would happen for him. Reluctantly, the doctors, nurses and probably the two sisters made the dreaded decision that all life support would have to be removed. His two sisters and the one daughter, his niece was on site that day. There his life ended on May 26, 1993. The family was saddened by this because everybody loved Timothy just as they did David and Joseph.

Timothy always had something funny to say even though he seemed to be a mean man to strangers. Long ago when Dave and his family visited the old schoolhouse for the summer, Timothy was not feeling very well and he was very snappy with them. It was probably the only time in his life that he really snapped at a relative. He also loved to drink his beer. Timothy told the baby girl, Bobbie, to go away and leave him alone. She was a loving child and kept the joy going. She went and got some peanut butter and said, "I am going to put some of this on your leg." She did just that and he sat there with the peanut butter on his leg and just laughed. Everybody remembered how happy was for the rest of the day. Everybody wondered how Bobbie made him laugh. Bobbie's sisters said, "Aw maybe it's because she likes beer too." Everybody thought that was very hilarious and teased Bobbie about that from then on. Even though at times he seemed to be a mean man to strangers, he was really deep down inside as nice as any person could be. The meanness was just a cover up for his pain.

Timothy's funeral was arranged by his eldest living brother, Samuel, Jr. Again, the church was full on that day, May 31, 1993 but it was kind of quiet. Mary's brother Thomas performed the eulogy for Timothy. It was not an easy thing for him to do since they grew up together years ago and they were very close. Nobody said any more about how Timothy died but a lot of people began to question why he had not been as careful as he usually was. The two sisters stayed on with Mama Julia and all of Joseph's children came by each day. Albertina didn't think that all of these people should come to the house as much as they did because she felt that it disturbed Mama Julia. This was so unlike Mama Julia not to want her family around. The family grew more concerned than ever, because Mama Julia was always so complacent that nothing ever seemed to disturb her.

In April of 1992 before Timothy died, the whole family was served a summons to court from Albertina's new attorney. It was quite a surprise to see such a notice coming from some one's own relative. The family had always been able to talk to one another in a loving way except for times when they had their own little sister and brother disputes. They were not able to talk to each other when Papa Samuel told them who would be the overseer of the remaining estate. Everybody was in an uproar about the sibling that Papa Samuel chose as the executor over the estate. He chose Dave because he cared deeply about the property and whether the taxes were paid in a timely manner. He also chose Dave because he knew that he would not let anyone take his estate from the family. He was absolutely correct because Dave did everything he could to keep the family happy and together. He collected all of the taxes from his sisters and brothers each year to make sure they were paid and up to date. It was very difficult getting his sisters and brothers to pay their part of the taxes without friction.

Needless to say nobody was in agreement with what Albertina wanted except for her sisters Lillie and Agnes. Everybody else was quite confused and tried very hard to help with settling this matter. The more they tried to help Albertina make wise decisions, the worse it got. Letters and telephone calls went all over the country. Still they couldn't get a complete understanding as to why they were being summoned to court. They found out later on that she wanted to build a house. It seemed liked the attorneys were making more of this than she planned to make of it. In reality the attorneys could do no more than she asked them to do. The contractors wanted her to have four acres to build on and everybody wondered why she needed that many acres just for one house and why they had to sign an incomplete form. The first thing that everybody thought was that these people could fill in any amount they wanted after they got everybody's signatures. The family members that didn't want to sign the form called their own attorney and found that their thinking was correct.

Since no one agreed on signing a blank form that could be filled out later by someone else, Albertina decided to live with her daughter in an apartment and Lillie went back home to Illinois. That was not going to be the last time that the family heard from her attorney though. Her attorney continued to send legal documents to the family practically trying to force them to sell their property. Of course, they didn't know who told the attorney to do this kind of act. It could have been anybody that was involved. The attorney tried to force the heirs of Papa Samuel to sign away their rights to the interest of Papa Samuel's estate. So the family members that didn't agree upon selling had to hire another attorney to write up a response explaining why they didn't want to sell their own property.

Albertina was still not completely clear on what had begun to happen but she had an idea because she called the ordeal a "war." It seemed that the Law was controlling everything, even the way the family began to talk to one another and the way they felt about one another. Mama "Grannie" Julia was at home, but all of this Law stuff was really confusing her. Her good health began to diminish little by little and she missed her son being there with her every day. Albertina continued to take care of her mother even though she was steadily working with her attorney about the heir property and to get her interest out of the estate. The family thought how can this be happening now and how could the attorney have such a strong hold on Albertina? He began to send the family more and more documents to be signed. Albertina's attorney's fees were mounting higher and higher. Still nothing else was changing with the estate because the law couldn't change anything unless everybody in the entire family agreed upon it. It was very hard for the family to keep a smile on their faces with other people and with each other because they didn't know who was against who and what.

CHAPTER 7:
A Tragedy For The Family

The family tried desperately to carry on with life in a normal fashion. It was very difficult because it seemed that evil was all over the family. Sickness and death was more than usual. One of the in-laws was so angry with the things that were going on, that he decided to send letters telling Albertina to stop fooling around with the Law because something bad was going to her. He said that Albertina and her sister were devils and that they caused evilness and that the estate was now cursed. Still for some reason the Law had her hooked and she was driven by some evil force to continue going to the courthouse and the attorneys. The situation had gotten to the point of no return and the attorney continued to do whatever he was told to do and he wasn't about to let up. He even paid a visit to the estate and walked all around the farm. The letters meant nothing to Albertina. She did not let the infamous letters bother her in the least bit. She also received infamous phone calls while she planned to sell the schoolhouse. She finally had to change the phone lines. She wouldn't let anyone take Mama Julia take to her church. Mama Julia loved going to church because she always enjoyed listening to the word and the gospel songs.

The situation kind of simmered down for a little while, but not for long. While the paperwork was still circulating to each family, Albertina was steadily making sure that the house was cleaned and she started throwing away everything that was old and looked like it meant nothing to anyone. The old schoolhouse was loaded with history books and antique furniture, but Albertina and her grandson really cleaned out all of those old treasures. They worked tirelessly. They threw away a lot of old papers, pictures, books, and old quilts that Mama Julia made by hand. Albertina and Lillie said to people that "Mama don't need all of this old stuff." They proceeded to tear down the "hen house" that Mama Julia had for a long time and she loved going outside to her back yard to get her eggs each day. Here was Albertina outside bare handedly tearing it down with the assistance of her own grandson. Mama Julia just looked with bewilderment and wondered what in the world was going on? Mama Julia was told to sit still on the porch and get some fresh air while it was nice outside. Albertina and her grandson also chopped down an apple tree, some rose bushes and finished off the peach tree that had been halfway destroyed by the ice storm in February of 1994. Albertina cleaned up the yard to make it look nice. Everybody wondered why she tore down Mama Julia's favorite little "hen house." Mama Julia was so upset that she would barely eat the food that Albertina prepared. She would look at the food as if something was wrong with it and turn away, but she would finally pick up her fork and start eating. Albertina ordered Mama Julia around the house as if she was a little toddler. Maybe it was because Mama Julia had a little bit of Alzheimer's disease. "Mama do this, Mama do that, Mama sit down, Mama be quiet," was all Mama Julia heard. Albertina wouldn't let her go outside to get firewood or go to check her mailbox which she was so accustomed to doing. Mama Julia really didn't need to walk across the street to the mailbox because the traffic was much faster than it was many years before. Mama Julia would go outside and just look out to the fields and not say a word to anyone. It was unbelievable but it was all in the best interest of Mama Julia because she was getting old and feeble according to the two sisters and their attorneys.

One day Mama Julia sat on her porch and anyone could see that she was getting yet a little older. She began to talk a little bit. She said, "I am goin to move to Memphis." Everybody looked at each other and said, "What is she talking about?" They asked her if she knew what she was talking about. They could tell that she really didn't want to leave her home but she thought that she was going to have a good time in the city of Memphis. Her grandchildren thought that she was a little bit confused and she didn't know what she was saying but the house did appear a bit empty that day. All of them went back inside the house and watched television. One of the grandchildren said, "Grannie, do you watch that show?" She answered with her little shaky voice, "Sometimes I watch it and that lady wears all those blonde wigs and that gold is not real." Then she chuckled. Albertina was sitting there and said, "Aw mama you don't know what you talking bout." Grannie said, "Yes I do to." Then Grannie said, "I am going to go and see my sister Judy." Everybody looked at each other and said, "Who is Judy?" Albertina said, "That was her sister that died many years ago." Everybody didn't know what to think about how Grannie's mind went into the past so suddenly like that.

Some of the neighbors began to whisper among themselves that Albertina was cleaning the house just to find the deed to the house because Mama Julia would not give up and tell her where it was. It was also rumored around town that the search was really on for the deed to the house so that they could sell the school house. None of the family members believed the rumor because of the source. They didn't know if this was reliable information or not. Sometimes cousin Earl sounded as if he was joking and other times it sounded true. Earl was one of the cousins on the other side of the Strong family.

The next thing the whole family knew was that Albertina was going to move Mama Julia out of the house and into the house with her daughter. All of a sudden after living in another apartment for about a year, they purchased a house and Mama Julia was there living with all of them. Mama Julia's great grandson used to always kick her for no apparent reason. Mama Julia had strong legs and it didn't bother her too much. The old schoolhouse was dark and empty. There was one little light left on the outside but it was still very dark around the house. Joseph's eldest son Matthew, stayed around the house as long as he could. He actually tried to get Albertina to let him rent the house instead of selling it to someone completely not related to the family. Albertina would not hear of it. At first he had a key to the house, but one night when he went to the house he found that all of the locks were changed. Her reason for wanting to sell the house was solely for Mama Julia's sake. She said, "Mama needs all of her money so that her health needs can be met. Besides, there are too many bad memories in this house." Mama

Julia was so healthy for her age, which was about ninety-nine at that time. She hardly ever had to go to the doctor. The truth of the matter was that Mama Julia didn't need any money, she was receiving more money and assistance than she could use.

Albertina and her family had a few choice people that they would let come and see Mama Julia that weren't relatives. So the relatives would go and visit the friends in order to see and talk to Mama Julia. Then the friends would take her back to Albertina's house. Mama Julia always asked if they could take her to the town in the country where her house was standing. It would almost bring tears to the family's eyes to have to tell her that the schoolhouse was not hers anymore and that she could not just go there whenever she got ready. Everything had been moved out of the house. Mama Julia was serious because and anyone could see in her face the disappointment when she didn't get to go to her own house.

Mama Julia could receive phone calls from her other grandchildren and family members but Albertina was always right there with her and listening to her conversations when Mama Julia was on the phone. Mama Julia's conversations were always short and sweet anyway. She usually said, "Yhello, Oh, I'm o.k. ha! ha! yeah yeah." Then her little voice would fade out to almost no sound at all. She never said good-bye or bye-bye or any kind of closing like that. She simply hung up the phone while the caller was still on the phone saying "hello, hello." It seemed as though she was hanging up in their faces. It was strange and funny at the same time. One day Carla called to see how her grandmother was doing. Albertina and her grandson were at home at the time. Somehow the conversation ended up in a big argument. Carla said something to the effect that Albertina was wrong in her plans of selling grandmother's house and that she was wrong in not letting the family visit Mama Julia. The conversation ended with them hanging up on each other. The grandson called Elizabeth on the phone and told her to tell Carla not to ever call their house again. Elizabeth became enraged and started calling him all kinds of ugly, bad names. She had never cursed at any of her relatives before then and she felt terribly bad about having to curse them but it was either that or trot over there and blow up or else they would never get to talk to their grandmother. She couldn't sit back and say nothing about the stupidity of it all.

It was not very long before the schoolhouse had a "For Sale" sign in front of it. Albertina told Matthew to remove all of his belongings from around the house. He had pigs, cows, horses, turkeys, ducks and his truck. Matthew ignored her. A few days later someone took the "For Sale" sign down and stepped on it. Then someone came and put it back up again. Some of the relatives said that the real estate agent contacted all of Albertina's living sisters and brothers and none of them disagreed with selling the house. There was no real proof of that though because the two brothers said that they did not agree with the sale. The sign kept going up and down until finally they decided to not even bother with the sign.

While at the same time that the house was in the process of being sold, legal documents were still coming to all of the family members about the property. It seemed as though someone was deliberately trying to confuse the whole family. All at the same time the family was still receiving documents about who they were and what new children popped up in the picture, children that no one ever heard of before. In other words they were illegal little bastards from other women. One woman claimed to have had a sexual relationship with Timothy and that she had a child with him but before he died he said, "I ain't never had a relationship of any kind with that woman." He also said that she drank a lot and that she got drunk too much for him and that she had relations with a lot of men. Her son was an illegal child, not knowing all of those years who his father really was. Then to add to the legal problems, along came some of Hanna's son's children that nobody really knew. This caused a big argument with the family. Hanna's son died about one year and a half after Dave, Joseph and their two nephews. He was with the children sometime and other times he was a single man with no children. Then also in the document for the estate sale comes along Agnes's deceased son's daughter. It looked like every time somebody died, more names were added to the list. Some of them could be proven and some of them could not be proven as legal heirs of the Samuel Strong estate.

The documents were getting longer and longer. Albertina's attorney seemed to enjoy every minute of it almost as if it was a chess game or something only he was going to get paid for it. Albertina began to accumulate more plaintiffs but some of them wanted to release the attorney that they had at that particular time. The problem with releasing him was that he wouldn't hear of being released. He wouldn't tell them how much money they owed him or anything. It was the biggest mess anyone could ever imagine.

The family began to wonder if Papa Samuel's other illegitimate child would have to be added to the heir list, even though she had not paid one penny for the taxes. Nobody had any idea how complicated this case could get until more attorneys became involved. The whole situation started out as an innocent desire to build a house turned out to be a complete nightmare. At the same time the real estate agent was working diligently to find a buyer for Mama Julia's schoolhouse. The agent said that she contacted some of Mama Julia's other children to see if she should go on with the sale of the schoolhouse. The other children said nothing about stopping the sale because they were thinking that this would solve the financial problem for Albertina to help with the medical and other needs. The schoolhouse did finally sell to a single Caucasian lady who was kind of afraid to stay there. She put up a big old gate and the only way anyone could get in was with a special card and a special number. She put a little sign up that said the "Old Strong School," which was a school for black children. It was nice of her to do that because this would mean that the schoolhouse would probably become a landmark someday. It would not be owned by the Strong family even though they bought it back from the school system. It would be owned by the people that bought it from Mama Julia who had owned it since the 1960's.

To drive by and look at the house only brought tears once again to the family and it made them very sad. Just to think that Mama Julia could have lived there a little longer and the family could have visited with each other just a little longer. It was so hard to get over the fact that the schoolhouse was gone from their lives forever. When

Matthew and Elizabeth got together one day on the rest of the farm, they began to reminisce about the good times that they used to have at the schoolhouse. They just stood there on the empty property and looked over the fence at the old schoolhouse. They became melancholy as they remembered the family members that used to come there every year. They asked each other over and over again, why did this awful thing have to happen? They knew that no one from any family would ever really want to experience what they were feeling at that point and time. They stood there and talked about how much they missed the family togetherness.

Later, Elizabeth went home and talked to her husband Edward about how she was feeling and that the loss of the schoolhouse was very painful. He said, "Maybe there was a reason why this happened. Maybe God had something better for the family." Elizabeth said, "Maybe you're right, maybe too many people were dying around there, maybe there would have been too many arguments over who was supposed to be the owner of the schoolhouse in the event that something happened to Mama Julia. Perhaps there was some good reason for it." To believe that that was the case would be the only way the family could get over the anguish, the depression, the sadness and the disappointment. Then some of the family members would say, "there could be nothing good to come out of this evilness, absolutely nothing." For one thing the last wish that Mama Julia had was that the schoolhouse not be sold. The only thing the Strong family could do was drive by and get a look at it and remember the good times that they once had there with the family and with Mama Julia.

It was still a blessing that the old schoolhouse was still standing. There were many times when the house could have been destroyed but by God's grace and mercy the school was still standing and only minor repairs were needed. All of the other black schools in that area had already been destroyed or other schools had replaced them. But the Strong schoolhouse was the original one since 1928. The neighbors had some of the classmates that went to the school were really upset that the schoolhouse was sold to someone that never went to that school, someone that could never know or feel the real history of the school.

All the new owner could know was what was told to her or what she read, which could have very well been incorrect information.

Ms. Bithers told the neighbors that she saw ghosts, heard the water running that no one had turned on, heard people talking in the house. It was said that Mama Julia used to love to run the water in the house even if she didn't need to. Papa Samuel died in the schoolhouse, so it was said that he may have been one of the ghost in the house that never left. No wonder Ms. Bithers was never at the house when people drove by. Elizabeth said that when she drove by the house she could feel the pit of her stomach knot up.

Some of the neighbors tried to welcome her into the neighborhood. She said a few words to them, but that was just about the extent of their conversations. She couldn't be neighbors with them because she was hardly ever there. Ms. Bithers told Albertina that she didn't think the neighbors and relatives liked having her around too much. Albertina said, "Not to worry about them because they did not understand how a white person could live in what once was a black home, a black school and how she could stand to live around black neighbors." Then she turned around and told Ms. Bithers to put a taller fence around the house so that she wouldn't be bothered about them. So that is exactly what Ms. Bithers did. Whenever someone wanted to go by the house, all they could see was the top of it and a little bit of the doors. The funny thing was that she didn't put a fence around the back where the view was the prettiest and the relatives could be seen even better.

The neighbors kept looking for the life that was once there, but there was virtually no life in the schoolhouse anymore. Thank goodness the rest of the Strong family on Papa Samuel's brother's side could still be found in their yards or on their porches and if one of the family members came by they had someone to talk to and visit with sometime. Thank goodness for Papa Samuel's nephew, who was still around with a little bit of life left at the ripe old age of ninety. He knew everything there was to know about the Strong schoolhouse and about the family history. He even had the bible that papa David Strong, the preacher had when he was alive and preaching. The bible was over a hundred years old and he wouldn't let anyone touch it. He did not mind the family coming to visit him for that good old family connection. Life went on even though Mama Julia's house was not where the family met anymore, even though her porch conversations were gone, and even though the family could not see her loving smile when they wanted to.

Mary was living right down the street from Mama Julia in the little house that Dave built before he passed away. She could see almost everything that went on around the house except for when she wasn't looking outside. She used to see Mama Julia sitting out on the porch sometimes all alone and wondered if she should go up and talk to her but she didn't want to get involved in any more of Albertina's business than she needed to. Mary wasn't feeling her best either. Rebecca came to live with her for a little while until she got herself a job and her own apartment. While she was there Mary became very ill and had to go to the hospital. Rebecca had noticed that Mary was not stable, could hardly stand up, and was falling down occasionally. The doctor said that she had a tumor in her colon and it had to be removed. She thanked the good Lord that it was benign. It was not easy explaining to her that she could not do the things that she used to do and take care of her own self at the same time. She could not understand that she was almost as ill as her husband was before he passed. The doctor was able to remove the tumor enabling her to carry on her normal activities for a while longer. It was decided by all of Mary's children that she could not live alone in the little house and do all of the things that needed to be done for a house. For some strange reason she couldn't get her bearings straight even though she had all of the money she needed to do whatever she wanted to do. All of her children believed that in her mind, she couldn't go on with her life without Dave.

Rebecca convinced her to move out of the tiny house into a bigger apartment with her. Mary stayed there comfortably except for the stairway which gave her a hard time because she wasn't supposed to do that much climbing. Because she was recuperating from her surgery, she was unable to clean house and cook as she usually did. Rebecca did most of the cooking and cleaning, but it really wasn't her forte. Rebecca felt that she was not a child and she wanted to go on dates and invite guest over. It was not easy to entertain guest and make sure that Mary was taken care of. They began to have serious arguments about this one little problem. Rebecca would leave and stay and Mary would worry about where she was even though she was a grown woman. They would argue about the bills, the late nights, and the cleaning. There was no way they could live together much longer even though Rebecca needed Mary to drive her places. Mary would rather drive Rebecca around than for Rebecca to drive her car. One day Rebecca wanted to go out on a date and she had bought a new red dress and red shoes. Everything was red. Mama Mary said, "Um, red on the floor." Everybody laughed. They just couldn't hit it off living together plus there was so much confusion. Mary wanted to live in her house where she didn't have to pay a house note or rent. When Mary felt that she was strong enough to move, she did just that.

When Mary moved to her house, she found that it wasn't quite what she wanted to do because her health began to fail again. She called her girls every day to let them know how badly she felt and that they would never understand how hard it was to live in pain until it happened to them. She said that her girls didn't care about what could happen to their mother. Of course, that was not what she truly felt, it was just her medication and illness that made her talk that way, if the truth be told.

Mama Josephine called her relatives and friends just to see how things were going in Tennessee. From several conversations, she finally realized that the old schoolhouse had been sold and nothing was the same anymore. Mama Josephine was not the same either. She had had some health problems and was in the hospital for quite some time. Mama Josephine was in her late eighties and doing pretty good living in her senior citizen flat in Wisconsin. She enjoyed her little flat, but she soon became too ill to live alone. Her daughter, Ellen, took care of her for a little while. Ellen's brother immediately took over the responsibility. Adam, Paul, and her baby Johnnie went to visit her for mother's day and she was very surprised and happy. They loved to video special events. So they videotaped her on that day. Every holiday was special to Mama Josephine and her children usually tried to either see her or call her as much as possible.

Springtime was very hot and it had already reached the ninety degree mark in June of 1995 and everybody was trying to get on with their lives even though the fast change in temperature interfered with the comfort of their daily routines. Albertina had done all she could to help with the care of Mama Julia. She took her to the doctor when she needed to go, took her to the store, and took her to the bank when she needed to cash her monthly social security check. Albertina even took care of all of Mama Julia's funeral arrangements in the event of her demise. Albertina bought Mama Julia a very beautiful headstone since she was about a hundred years old.

Everything seemed to be going just fine, but one day Mary received a telephone call from Albertina. Albertina told her that she was going to the doctor to check on something about herself. The next thing Mary knew was that Albertina was admitted into the hospital for some infection that she had in her body. Albertina stayed in the hospital for a little while and was then released. She went home and continued her usual duties but for a while no one heard from her even though she was still working on the partition or sale of the estate. Fourth of July, Birthdays, Thanksgiving, Christmas and New Year's day had gone by and a new year-1996- was about to begin when one night while sitting at the table that used to be in Mama Julia's house, Albertina just laid her head down and went to sleep. When she was discovered by her children, they found that she was not alive. When the news finally hit the rest of the family, it was quite shocking because nobody knew she was that sick. They figured she was as healthy as an ox since she was doing all of this legal work with her attorneys. The arrangements were made and only the family attended her funeral because not very many people were made aware of her death. The family was really concerned about Mama Julia mainly because Albertina had been taking care of her so the question was what were they going to do now?

Mama Julia stayed there with Albertina's daughter, Geneva, her husband, her grandson, Brandon and her great grandson DeMarcus for a little while, but Samuel, Jr. soon moved Mama Julia in with him and his wife and took care of her for a little while. Mama Julia was now a hundred and she was really not herself especially after the environmental change and she was getting feeble. Samuel, Jr. and his wife would buy her new underwear and clothes, place them where they belonged and when they went to get them for her, they discovered that Mama Julia had removed them and put them somewhere else because she said that she didn't want them anyway. She was also still having a problem with going to the restroom and she would not keep underwear shields on for protection against accidents. She would do little things and keep a smile on her face as if she knew what she was doing. Samuel, Jr. was not sure what to do for her and it hurt him to see this happening to his mother. He hated it with a passion, but since they didn't have someone there to see to her needs all day they pondered over the idea of placing her in a nursing home. One night when the family was sitting at the dinner table eating, Mama Julia fell to the floor and her son, John, picked her up and carried her to the bedroom. They panicked because they thought she had expired at that very instance.

A whole year had passed again since Albertina had passed away but Mama Julia was still going. Since Samuel, Jr. didn't know how he was going to handle juggling his schedule with taking care of his mother he regretfully came to the decision to let her try the nursing home for a little while and if it just didn't work they would bring her home and bring a nurse to the house to take care of her. They did all they could from day to day along with their own daily schedules.

It was a very cold day for Mama Julia in the nursing home up north. The snow was about seven inches deep and it was white and beautiful because not very many cars had made tracks in it. It seemed as if everything was alright and everything was taken care of but that was not the case. The family received a call late night January 30, 1997 that Mama Julia had expired. The family was saddened by this news, but they also had mixed feelings. Some expected it to happen while others were not ready for it to happen yet. There was still so much she could have told her grandchildren and great-grandchildren but never had the opportunity to do so. There was nothing but love in their hearts for her.

She looked so beautiful at her "home going" celebration, all dressed in white. Samuel, Jr. gave the eulogy and her other son, John did the remarks along with other friends. The funeral was held at the same church as Dave and Joseph. Many friends and relatives were there and all kinds of flowers positioned along the walls of the church. After the funeral was over everybody gathered around and had dinner together as they talked about some of the good old days and met with their friends and relatives that they hadn't seen for many years.

Almost two years had pased since Albertina had expired and some of the problems had kind of simmered down only to be disturbed once again by her attorney who sent each family member another document. He probably didn't realize that he was disturbing the peace that the family was enjoying at that time. They would have been very happy not receiving another document. This document stated that the plaintiffs wanted to get a conservator for the illegal and unknown children of the family. When the defendants read the documents, names were found that no one recognized. Naturally the defendants began to ask questions about who those people were. Some of the names were made up by some of the plaintiffs in the family. They even began to look at the good side and speculated that maybe it was a way to hold up any unwanted progress that could have been made in the future or maybe even that someone was thinking that they could make a deal with an unknown and get part of their said interest. Even though everybody knew that more than likely a deal like that would never be successful because usually if someone gets something free they are not about to let it go to someone else even if they did make a verbal agreement.

Another thing that was interesting about the document was that it was signed by Albertina's daughter and grandson. This time the family had come to their wits end. They called a meeting and of course everybody didn't show up to the meeting, but they went on with the people that were there. The question came up about the document and immediately Albertina's daughter and grandson acted like they didn't know what the family was talking about this time. They wanted to act innocent even after all that had happened. Everybody could see on their faces that they knew they had been up to something.

Albertina's grandson said, "Well all my grandmother wanted to do was build a house and what was wrong with that?" Albertina's grandson, Jed didn't understand that there were more people involved in this heritage than his own grandmother and that all paperwork must be in order before any agreement could be made and it was clear that the paperwork wasn't written to accommodate her wants. The family agreed that there was absolutely nothing wrong with building a home it's just that it had to be done correctly. So they were back at square one again with both attorneys going back and forth and the defendants using every tactic they could think of to delay any action from taking place. Something had to be done. The family was just pulling at straws.

After they had dinner they discussed what they wanted to do. There were about three or four different suggestions. Some wanted to keep all of the estate for sentimental reasons and some wanted to sell all of the estate and be done with all of it, taxes, upkeep and all. Some wanted to put a road on the property for access to each person's interest and to let each person do what they wanted to do with their own. Something like the developers did to other properties. "No, that won't work either," said Samuel, Jr. "Some of the family would end up in the back and that would be unfair and we want to be fair about this," said John. Lillie then stood up and said something that seemed a little crazy to some of the family members. Lillie said, "Nobody knows about this estate like I do because I worked on it for years." Everybody looked at her and wondered why she would believe that she was that important. Later they found out that she was the only one that Papa Samuel had actually ever signed over part of the property. She was married at that time and her husband went crazy on her so she left the little house given to her by Papa Samuel.

When Papa Samuel found out what went on, he set the place afire so that the crazy husband couldn't live there either. Her crazy husband wasn't so crazy after all because he collected some kind of insurance money and went on about his business. Maybe that was why Lillie said what she said. Maybe she had some kind of a bad flashback or something. John comforted her by saying, "Tell us all about it big sister." The next suggestion was that maybe they could get a developer and develop the estate which some of the family members had already talked about, where everybody could benefit from the proceeds. No. That was not an option either. Cousin Jake said, "For one thing that is too damned expensive, who has fifty thousand dollars in here?" Mama Mary was there and she said, "Yeah, it probably cost a pretty penny." It appeared that the older children were set on selling everything and leaving it for the children and grandchildren was strictly not an option as far as they were concerned.

More and more questions were raised about the legal documents, still there was no answer as to who the boy was that seemed to be a mystery that nobody really knew about. No one really knew why Albertina added his name to the inheritance list but one thing was for sure, nobody knew anything about this child. The rest of the family began to wonder why in God's name anyone would want to put someone's name on a legal document if he was not known to the family as a relative. They wondered who knew this mysterious child and who was he friends with? Was someone trying to make him feel as if he was a part of the family? Timothy never talked about this mysterious child, never visited with him, never introduced him to the family nor did he ever claim him. The family was thoroughly confused at this point because if this was a legal child someone would have known about him a long time ago.

When Mama Julia died late in 1997 oddly enough, the mysterious child appeared at the funeral and Jake took him around to the family trying to confirm that his mother was correct in adding him to the inheritance but some of the family members thought what in the world is he doing. They felt really uncomfortable considering the circumstances. Some of the older relatives were saying, "Yeah that's his child alright." Some of the younger relatives were saying, "That is not his child and if he is he needs to prove it because Timothy never brought him around us." Nevertheless they spoke to him and kept on about their business which was to respect their deceased Mama Julia. They would think about the mysterious grown man at some other time. No one heard from or saw him again after the funeral, but his name was still on the legal documents and the attorney still claimed to represent him in the law suit. Even though the defendants wrote letters to their attorneys to explain that they did not know this young man, the plaintiff's attorney insisted upon keeping the young man on the interrogatories and responses. The attorney had no proof except for the mother's word that this child was a relative of the Strong family.

The law suit began to get more and more confusing as each attorney did everything they could to keep the case hung up in court which was what the family wanted to do at first, considering the fact that Mama Julia owned one third of everything before she died. Other children's names slowly appeared in the case as some of the relatives passed on. The longer the list became, the more mixed up the names became. It seemed as though the case would never come to an end. With all of the confusion, the family could only pray because that was the only thing that could bring them out of this much confusion, especially a family that once loved each other and would stop at nothing to stay together as a loving family. So they struggled to stay on an even keel while some of the older relatives would say very ugly things to cover up for the hardship that they had put upon the family. Instead of taking the blame, they would say things like, "The children of the deceased children should not get any of the inheritance," even though the deed said that the property would belong to all legal heirs, fee simple absolute. They said things like, "None of this would have happened like this if Mary, Samuel, Jr., and John hadn't gotten together and got their own attorney." The older relatives just couldn't face the reality that in order to keep what was rightfully theirs, they had to fight for it or else some strange person would have it for little or nothing. For ten long years the family feud continued. Not knowing that this struggle started long ago with David, Joseph, Albertina, Lillie, Timothy, John, Samuel, and Hanna, the younger children thought that ten years was just way too long and they did not have the time or patience to wait any longer. The town was growing by the minute with million dollar homes springing up all around them. It was beginning to look more like the city rather than the fresh open country they were used to visiting. Most of them would never be able to afford such expensive living conditions as that anyway. It was the topic of every conversation they had for ten years. When they talked to each other it wasn't, how are you doing today? It was, "Have you heard anything from the attorneys?" Everyone's hopes were that this would all soon come to an end. The older relatives still wanted to sell everything and the young ones still wanted to keep it for the sake of sentimental values because it had been in the family for ninety-seven years plus.

The meeting ended with a vote on whether to sell or not to sell. From what everybody could tell the vote was to sell. Before anyone could say anything else, the meeting was adjourned and everybody was getting up from their seats. Still no one said anything about the mystery boy. It was as if someone was withholding information from the rest of the family. The very next day, a sign was in front of the property saying "FOR SALE." It was a hard pill to swallow for some of the family to look at the sign standing there for the whole town to see. A few people inquired about the property but their offers were not very good. Some of the offers were just plain ridiculous as far as the defendants were concerned. They felt that the property was worth much more than they were offering because the property meant so much to them since they had had it in the family for about one hundred years. It was as if they wanted to pay absolutely nothing and get something that the family cherished for ninety odd years.

CHAPTER 8:

The Buyers And The Families

O ne day John and Samuel received a call from a very nice man who was an attorney and apparently money was no object for him. He wanted to purchase the property for his daughter and son-in-law. They did not want to change the beauty of the property. They wanted to build a house on it and have an organic farm, unlike what most of the prospective buyers wanted to do. Most of the prospective buyers wanted to buy the property and make a big profit from it by building many houses on it and then selling them for outrageous prices. All of the family members began communicating either by telephone or letters to find out what each one thought of this nice person that wanted to buy the property even though some of them still were not going to sell their inheritance. They all decided to go on with the prospect's offer. When they received the contract, they had many more questions. At first they thought that the prospective buyers had not offered enough money per acre. There were some clauses in the contract that many of the family members could not agree upon. Back to the drawing board they went. Another contract was prepared that was more agreeable even though they did not remove one of the clauses that was very restrictive. Also, some of the family members decided that they absolutely did not want to sell any of the property and that they wanted to draw up a completely different contract. They wanted the contract to state exactly who wanted to sell and exactly who did not want to sell because the contract would probably never have gotten signed if they had not determined who wanted to do what with their own inheritance.

The buyers were nice enough, rich enough or either knew the right people to make another contract to state exactly who wanted to sell and who did not want to sell. The writing of an agreeable contract took approximately two years. Everybody was beginning to think that the buyers would not continue with the deal and that they would go on to another seller since there were many sellers in that particular area. Since the buyers did not seek another seller the family began to think that the buyers were trying to play them for a bunch of fools and that the buyers thought they could offer anything they wanted.

They learned through other sellers and buyers that some people were selling their land for twice as much as they were and at times, three times as much. The older family members were anxious to get the whole deal done and over with. They said things like, "Go on and sign the contract, that's all you need to do, you don't even have to read it." Of course, they got some static from the younger generation because most people just don't sign contracts without reading what's in them even if they are related to each other.

Time continued to go on and more of the family died leaving more grandchildren to add to the contract. One day a contract was mailed to the family with a complete list of who wanted to sell and who did not want to sell. The real estate agent was very persistent. He even brought some of the family members together to look at the map to see just what could happen and what other options they had. He then called other members long distance to have conference calls to discuss the possibilities. It was so smooth the way he handled the business of securing engineers to come out and complete a survey the property which described every square foot. They all joked around and had a good meeting. The real estate agent even offered to put another pond on the property just for one of the cousins that couldn't accept the fact that the pond would belong to someone else. The pond had always been a quiet retreating place for him and he was really serious about them putting another pond on the property that he wanted to keep. Of course, the real estate did not see that he was serious, so he assumed that it was a joke. All at the same time the attorney's fees were mounting up and the family was wondering who was going to pay them. A few more months passed and the contract was signed by all thirty family members. It was unbelievable that the contract had gotten almost to the point of completion. A date was set to meet with the real estate attorney to sign all of the deeds that were prepared. Family members came from out of town to close the sale. Everybody was sitting around the big oval table signing all of the papers when all of a sudden a fax came through. It was from the plaintiff's attorney stating that he would not sign for the sale to close because he was still representing the mysterious boy and he was not included in the contract. They were all sitting there ready and waiting to finally sign the contract to sell part of their inheritance, only the alleged son was not mentioned anywhere in the contract. The attorney simply could not let go of the case. Then all hell broke loose with the plaintiff's attorney who was hired by Albertina at first, somehow now he was representing the unknown child. Everybody in the office was fit to be tired at that point.

Rebecca stood up and said, "Oh no, that Albertina has come back from the dead and is still trying to cause problems." Thank God, she had not really come back or they would all have thought they were losing their minds. "It is a shame to say this, but we were blessed when God decided it was time for her to leave us alone, said Elizabeth." "We knew nothing good would come of her selling Mama Julia's house and acting like it was all hers and hers alone. We can't stand that attorney of hers because he acts like everything is personally his," said Bobbie. "Just because she wanted to build a house and sell Mama Julia's land and if the truth be told, she didn't want anybody to profit from it but her and her children. Her impatience turned into greed," said Matthew. The devil was truly working against the family through her. It was so bad that she sold all of Mama Julia's belongings and threw away all of her treasured letters, notes, pictures, address book, receipts, antique furniture, and antique jewelry. Mama Julia even had an antique telephone in her house.

"After the devil, so to speak, got all of that stuff done he made her go back to the lawyer again and get some more papers written up for the lawsuit," said Elizabeth. Then the defendants went back to their lawyer again and it continued on like that for several years. Back and forth, back and forth, back and forth, she went to her lawyer and the defendants went back and forth to their lawyer. She went to her lawyer again and they went to their lawyer again, just like a pendulum. It was so mind boggling for all of them and so physically tiring that it was hard for the family to carry on a normal daily life.

They began to whisper amongst one another, saying that that old Albertina should never have involved the alleged son's name in the lawsuit and that they couldn't stand that old attorney that she hired. They thought that it must be some kind of an omen brought on by Albertina's actions. They joked around saying that Albertina had come back from the dead to make sure they didn't get any of Timothy's part of the property. One of David's daughters said, "She can't do any more damage because our daddy is kickin her butt and she is saying, oh I'm sorry, please forgive me." "Albertina has already messed things up by selling Mama Julia's schoolhouse, why would she come back from the dead and mess up something else?" said John. Everybody chuckled but when the plaintiff's attorney faxed the information about leaving out a child that nobody knew it really slowed up the progress. Everybody just put their pens down and prepared to leave the office but nobody knew what they were going to do next. They buyer's attorney said that something like that happened to him one time. A child came up from out of nowhere and they quickly disclaimed her. He was trying to comfort the sellers because they were really about to give up on the whole shebang.

They went home and slept over it. The buyers were very persistent and would not let the sellers rest. They made arrangements with the defendants' attorney to prepare a motion to approve the ones that wanted to sell and also approve the ones that want to keep their inheritance. At first, the defendants' attorney did not seem to want to get involved or he was preoccupied with another case, but he went along with it for the defendants' sake. He could sense the frustration. He was very successful in at least getting the sale approved in the courts. Some of the plaintiffs were very happy with the outcome and some of them were dissatisfied because they didn't realize how little money they were going to get after it was all said and done. They thought they should have gotten more money that very day but the mysterious child situation was still not resolved. Needless to say some of the family members walked away from the courtroom, with half frowns and half smiles on their faces. They could not understand why the judge did not rule on this that very day in the courtroom. Why did they have to drag this out linger than need be? What was the holdup? After all, it had already been ten years of fighting a lawsuit. It was decreed by the judge that the money would be placed in an escrow account for the alleged son. Everybody began to wonder why on earth they put money in an escrow account for a child that nobody knew.

After the first part of the sale was finalized, the buyers offered to buy more of the property. The family members that wanted to keep Inheritance for time being were still upset about the buyers putting a stipulation in the contract saying that they would have the "first right of refusal" meaning that the owners couldn't sell unless the buyers agreed. This really did not sit well as far as the some of the owners were concerned. They felt that if the law could fix it that way then the law could do almost anything to what they owned, so they decided that they would rather just get out of the whole situation. Of course, some of the owners had to really think about the new clause in the contract and they were not ready at that moment to make a decision. It had already been very emotional to sit and watch some of their family members sell what their grand and great father had worked so hard to keep for their children. On the other hand, this was the best answer for the family. There were too many people in the family to make use of the property and still be up to code standards with city planning and development. The other option would have been to subdivide which would cost a preposterous amount and nobody in the family had that much money to make the property accessible for everybody's use. They pondered and they pondered over what to do about their inheritance. They wondered why they struggled so hard for the little bit of money that they stood to get if they sold their inheritance that had a longtime family history.

Even though part of the Strong family was struggling with selling part of their inheritance, some of the Strong family got together and planned a family reunion. They really hadn't had one since 1975 and twenty-five years had passed and so much had happened. They thought this would be a good way to try to get their minds off their problems. Many babies had been born and many grownups had passed, many had become seriously ill, and some had become drug addicts and night carousers. Not everybody was bad though, some of them had gone off to college and gotten degrees and gotten married. Sure enough things were not the same as it was twenty-five years ago. Even the neighborhood had grown considerably.

When everybody finally made it to Cousin Andrew's house they were ready to fellowship with each other and enjoy the feast that had been prepared for them overnight. T-shirts with their grandmother and grandfather's picture and names were on the shirts. Booklets were given to the family with their names and their birthdates. Cameras were flashing all over the place and a whole hog was cooked outside, along with ribs, chicken, steaks, hamburgers, franks, baked beans, fish, scratch cakes, slaw, corn on the cob and drinks. There was one thing different about this particular reunion from most other reunions. Most of their reunions were held in the summer like an outdoor luncheon. This reunion was held in the fall and it was very cool outside. Since it was so blazing hot in the summer, they decided to have the reunion in the fall when it was usually kind of cool and still kind of warm. Tents were set up all over the estate. Everybody began to gather around the tables of food. They smiled at one another and tried to say only good things about each other but deep down inside they really wanted to talk about the terrible things that had happened to the family and jump down each others' throats. They began to think about why they had not been together in such a long time and as the evening fell upon them they noticed that it was extremely chilly for a fall day in the south. They found themselves putting on winter coats and winter hats at the family reunion. The weather was most unusual for autumn.

Mama Mary wanted so much to attend the family reunion and visit with her relatives and friends but she had visited the south just a month before the reunion. She had to go back up north because she was also scheduled to see her doctor around the same time. Everybody tried to convince her to skip this doctor's visit and stay for the family reunion but she simply did not want to miss her appointment at that time even though she dreaded the doctor's visits. She did get to visit some of her very close family members before she went back to Ohio which was good.

Everybody ate and chatted for quite awhile, then they went home or to their hotel rooms to rest for the second part of the reunion that was arranged for the next day. It was not like it was twenty-five years ago when the family commenced to moved from one house to the other on the same street and convene again only at one of the other cousins estate. Back then, some of them would just stay at one of the other houses until the next day. They especially loved going to Mama Julia's house to sit and visit until the wee hours of the night. They couldn't do that because some of them including Mama Julia had sold their houses to other people and there was no way they could go to those houses and spend the night. The new owners would think they were really strange people. Some of them went out on the town for a little while. They usually did that when they had company from out of town. Something else was very different about this reunion. Mama Julia was not there, Papa David was not there, Timothy was not there, Joseph was not there, Albertina was not there, Agnes was not there, Pops was not there, Peaches was not there, and Torrence was not there. When they got together and began to reminisce about the good old days and the good days to come.

Elizabeth, Carla, Rebecca, Bobbie and Geoffrey were very concerned about their mother. Mary had fallen very ill around March. She had gone to the doctor several times but they had not really diagnosed the problem. Mary had started to lose a lot of weight which was very abnormal for her because she had always been healthy and weighed two hundred or more pounds. To see her down to one hundred and sixty pounds so soon was devastating. These were perilous times for the children. Seeing their mom so very ill and at the same time trying to keep a business mind when communicating with their attorneys and the buyers of their inheritance. The doctor said that she was doing fine but would not explain the weight loss to her children. When her daughter took her to the doctor one day, the doctor immediately admitted Mary to the oncology area of the hospital. That meant that they were dealing with cancer. It was called carcinoid cancer. She was in so much pain that she could not talk on the phone without moaning and groaning. She felt so much better after her short stay in the hospital. Her doctor started treatments for this cancer so that she could continue to live a somewhat normal life. The treatments were not easy for her to take. She would become nauseated, she would get diarrhea, her equilibrium was thrown off and she was in excruciating pain. She was so uncomfortable even though she had a nice bed and quiet surroundings. Surprisingly she could still get up and drive a car if she really needed to go somewhere. She prayed day and night and went long distances so that preachers could pray for her and anoint her with oil.

All of Mama Mary's children were having a difficult time in general trying to go on with life and face the fact that their mother was very ill. Elizabeth found comfort in going on extensive shopping sprees, Bobbie spent a lot of time traveling and going to casinos, Carla spent a lot of time shopping and casinos, Rebecca drank more alcohol, shopped extensively, and went to the casinos. Rebecca had a good male companion and one day he noticed that her new truck had been in some sort of an accident. The whole front bumper had been knocked off and there were several dents. When he asked Rebecca about it, she didn't want to tell him. When she found out that it would cost a pretty penny to fix it, she asked him to help her. He agreed to help her and then he found out that the whole steering column was demolished. The question rose up again. He asked, "Rebecca, how did you do all of this to your truck and not report it to the police or anyone?" She finally admitted that she had been drinking heavily that night and drove the truck into a ditch. Everybody was flabbergasted for a little while. A few months later, she ran her new S.U.V. into some kind of an object but she quickly had the dent removed so that nobody would ask her about it.

Mama Mary continued to lose the weight and it even frightened her. She constantly talked about her carcinoid tumors and her liver, all at the same time keeping her composure and giving other people the impression that she was doing fine. When her pain was just too excruciating she stopped driving her car and allowed relatives to drive her around. On December the twelfth, she went shopping and brought a few things. This made her feel better just to be able to do a little something on her own. It also made her children feel as though there was some hope that she really was doing just fine. But, soon after that her voice began to diminish slowly and talking for a long time was out of the question. Her body grew weaker and weaker. A little thing like getting up to use the restroom was something she never imagined to be an impossible task to do. She finally decided to wear protective underwear to avoid accidents at bedtime or any other time. The pain grew more and more piercing. The pain was so strong that sometimes she was found on her knees in her bed. This somehow relieved some of the pain. She didn't like for anyone to disrupt anything that she thought she could take care of. The tumor in her colon made her feel as though she needed to defecate all of the time. When anyone tried to help walk her to the restroom, she would fuss with a pointed finger and say, "You see, I don't need to be here with everybody, that's why I need to do everything myself. Everybody just smiled and said, "That's o.k. mom, you can stay here with us and let us help you if you want to."

One evening at her own home, she decided that she wanted to cook a chicken. It was a whole chicken and it had to be cut into pieces. As she was cutting it up, she became very weak and slowly fell to the floor. Geoffrey happened to be in the kitchen too and picked her up and carried her back to bed. She woke up and smiled at him and said, "You are really trying to help me aren't you, Geoffrey?" He said, "Yes mama, I am." Of course, the rest of the family was notified and they all wanted her to go immediately to the hospital. Mama Mary did not want to go to the hospital because she was certain that the medicine she was taking every month was not helping her and that she would probably not get to go back home. Everybody was at a loss for words. All they could do was cry and try to explain what was happening and wonder if there was something that could be done to relieve Mama Mary from her pain.

Mary convinced everybody that she was going to be fine and everybody that she was going to be fine and decided to stay home. She had a knack for being very convincing when she wanted something. This lasted for about one week. Just as she was getting up one morning the same feeling came upon her again. She fell once again, only this time there was a small cut on her head. The blood from the cut frightened her and that settled it for her. She decided it was time to go to the hospital for care. When she arrived at the hospital, the staff immediately admitted her to the oncology section again. Her weight continued to drop pound by pound because she could not eat anything and keep it down. They gave her some medicine to ease the pain and it made her drowsy. She called her children and told them to hurry up and get there even though they were out of town. She told them that she had a room full of folks on day and that lifted her spirits. She was happy and you could hear the laughter and smiles in her voice. When her daughters got there, she looked up and said, "It took you an awfully long time to get here." They replied with, "We got here as soon as we could Mama, we're sorry that we're late."

Mary's doctors came in and the family talked with them for several hours. Both of her doctors were very patient and gentle with the family and you couldn't help but to respect what they were doing for Mama Mary. They had an idea as to what was going to happen but there had been times when they were wrong. Of course, those times were absolute miracles. Mary's sisters, brothers and children were standing on the word of God and hoping for a miracle that she would come out of this illness and continue on with her life here on earth for a while longer.

The doctor ordered a Barium Enema Test and N.G. Tube. They wanted to check and see if whatever it was that was causing her food not to stay down could be removed. The testing was unsuccessful but she did receive the enema. The enema irritated her and made her uncomfortable. She was feeling so bad that she told one of her daughters to "get lost." Of course, there was nothing they could do at that point because the tumor in her colon had grown so very large and it was continually growing. Her kidneys were failing also, to the point that her body would not release the fluids. The doctor then ordered a catheter. Mama Mary refused to allow them to give it to her. The nurse begged and pleaded for Mary to let her insert the catheter. Mama Mary replied, "I know my body and I do not want it." She simply did not want that thing in her body and she proved it by going to the restroom on her own. When she got up out of her bed and walked around, everybody in the hospital room was astonished.

Mama Mary had already told all of her children that she knew she was leaving and that she wouldn't be on this earth very much longer. Naturally, her children, her friends, and her relatives did not want to believe such a thing was going to happen, because she was extremely loved even though she did not acknowledge that fact. She had witnessed so many of her own friends and family with this similar illness, two of them were her best friends including her husband David. The loss of those close friends and relatives really left her feeling alone and empty. It was a marvelous wonder that she could go on as long as she did with her own illnesses. She remembered all of the good times they had together. This kind of illness had happened to her loved ones so often in her life that she even had an idea about what was going to happen to herself even though she didn't want it to happen. It seemed as though she was telling herself to face the reality that not many people ever want to face. Not many people would allow themselves to even think like that let alone accept the loss of a loved one or a friend. It took intelligence and a strong will to be able to handle so many losses in nearly the same way including, her illness.

Even though Mama Mary was getting up walking around and saying a few things, the pain continued to grow and many small doses of morphine were injected. The N.G. tube was also added to help the suction of excess fluids from her stomach. The fluid was very dark, like coffee. Her daughters were all there taking turns staying up, hoping, and praying that her condition would get better.

They were thinking that everything was going to be just fine, especially when Mary told two of her girls to go to the bank and get Geoffrey's money out of the bank, pay the car insurance and the light bill for her. The girls looked puzzled when Mama said these things to them and they hesitated to move on this order. It didn't do them much good to hesitate, because Mama Mary told them again to go ahead and do what she told them to do. Again, they looked at each other in bewilderment and wondered why she was worrying about such things at this time. Mama Mary told them again in a very firm tone to take care of these things, only this time she sounded angry because the girls seemed to be ignoring her request. They finally went to the bank and got the money.

When they returned to the hospital room, she asked to see the money and then asked if it was all there? She ordered her girls to give her the money so that she could count it. Mama Mary was so week and she tried desperately to appear as though she was able to at least count money. Then she calmly laid the money down as if to say that there was no more need in trying to do anything. This was a bit much for the girls to bear and they were very hurt, so they became angry also and told their mother that she knew better than to have all of that cash in the hospital room. Why, she herself had taught the girls not to have that much cash in those rooms because people can come in and ramble through the patients things and take them. The girls could only blame their mother's unwillingness to argue with them like she used to, on her illness and the medication.

It was strange because for one minute the patient was fine and the next minute there was absolutely no response, they just couldn't believe what was happening. Just the week before Mama Mary had called family and friends while in the hospital and talked for short periods. The next week she couldn't call or talk to anyone.

A social worker came to the room to discuss the options that were available for Mama Mary. The decision was to have a nurse come to the house and take care of her at home with equipment, medicine and the insurance would take care of her medical bills. This sounded good to everybody. At least she would be taken care of around the clock.

Friends, relatives and family continued to pray and visit Mama Mary. She woke up for a few minutes when her neighbor came by and she smiled at her. Mama Mary listened to everybody that came and talked in her room. A preacher came in and she heard him talking. She woke up for a minute and said in a very low, soft and soothing whisper, "Who is that talking?"

One of the days during Mama Mary's stay in the hospital, Bobbie entered the room with one of Mama Mary's new sweaters on. Bobbie had gone through Mama Mary's clothes at the house and decided to freshen up and put on a clean change of clothes before she went back to the hospital. When Mama Mary gazed up from her sleep and rubbed her face as if she was feeling healthy. She looked up and said, "Hey, take my sweater off." It took everybody in the room to decipher what she said. Everybody looked at each other and wondered why she was so worried about her sweater at a time like this while she was in the hospital. Again, they began to think that Mama Mary was going to be just fine. The room was filled with laughter. Mama Mary was not laughing with them. Then reality set in with her daughters that this was an extremely serious matter. Not so much the sweater but the whole situation at hand. It seemed normal because she always said funny things and she never laughed at her own jokes. It was very cold that day in Ohio which was usual for January. The snow began to fall and it was so pretty but it only lasted for a short while which was quite unusual for that area.

CHAPTER 9:

Depositions In The Law Office

J ust at the same time that everybody was concerned about Mama Mary's illness, the defendant's attorney was about the business of making arrangements to question the alleged son of timothy in his office. When the attorney asked the alleged son where his supposed father was buried, he answered arrogantly, the he didn't know. The witnesses looked at each other and said, "What a sin and a scandal, he doesn't even know where his supposed father's body is but he wants to claim his money." When they questioned the alleged son's mother, she knew just about everything. She said that Timothy was crippled with arthritis and then she asked the attorneys to confirm that she was correct, "Isn't he?" The attorney then asked how old they were when she became pregnant with his baby. She said, with a cocky attitude, "Oh, we were nineteen and we were boyfriend and girlfriend." She said that he was the only one during that time. She then said, "Of course, I now have four other children with my last name and they are not Timothy's children."

The attorneys seemed to fall for her deposition because she said under oath that Timothy was the only man that she had forty-eight years ago, but she never claimed Timothy as the father on the birth certificate or on any school records. Nothing was on paper with a father's name on it. The mother said that Timothy even came to the hospital to see her when she delivered the baby boy. The question was still in the minds of the family, why on earth didn't he claim the boy and why on earth didn't she make any claims with Timothy until now? Forty-eight years had passed and Timothy could have used a son in his life but this boy never visited or made himself visible until after Timothy died and why did Aunt Albertina add his name on the lawsuit? It was all a mystery to the family, especially this family because if it was supposed to be known about any child being born to the family, it surely would have been known before forty-eight years had gone by.

While Mama Mary was in the hospital, the case was still going on in the South about the alleged son of Timothy. The attorneys made the decision together to go ahead and have the DNA testing done and they would use the escrow money to pay for it. Elizabeth was the contact person for the defendant's attorney and she was practically making the decisions for the family to agree with having the DNA testing. Of course, they would have to present this decision to the court and the Chancellor would have to decree the petition. Before Mama Mary went into the hospital, she was informed about this DNA and she said, "I don't know why they should do all of this because Timothy never claimed that boy as his son." The attorneys couldn't find any records proving that he was the son of Timothy. Mama Mary said that the boy's mother was lying about this child and she was very adamant about it. Still the attorneys continued to say that the unknown child could possible make a claim for the money and they had no idea which way this part of the case could go. This left the family with not much of a choice about agreeing with the DNA testing.

The family had used a total of seven attorneys, three attorneys out of the state and the Chancellor for ten years and still couldn't resolve the problem. The Football player and the Case of two brothers cases were settled long before the Strong case was finalized. Even King-of-pop case had been settled out of court.

Finally a contract was signed to sell part of the inheritance, only again the alleged son's name was not included in the contract. Then all hell broke loose with the plaintiffs' attorney who was hired by Albertina at first, but somehow now he was representing the unknown child. The whole case continued to be one big miserable nightmare. Nobody wanted to disown a relative but at the same time everybody felt betrayed by Albertina, Lillie and their attorney. Most importantly, the family felt that Timothy had been betrayed by his family. After all, what business was it of his sisters to report to an attorney about a grown up child that never said two words, hi or bye, to any of the family until he was told by his mother that he could possibly reap the monetary benefits that even Timothy could not have. Unless, of course, she as going to benefit from it herself. The question popped up in all of their minds, where on earth did the alleged son's mother get the nerve to start acting as though she had always been in touch with Timothy? Timothy was always alone, never on the phone with anyone, never wrote a letter, and always on his porch alone. All he wanted was a friend and a companion to be around him. He was always happy when someone came to see him.

The family was so frustrated that they began to wonder why the attorneys just didn't go ahead with the hearing and let voices from both sides be heard. It seemed as though both of the attorneys believed that this boy was actually the son of Timothy. John being the optimistic person that he was said, "Maybe the attorneys wanted them to hope for the best and expect the worst." The defendants began to feel as though they were fighting a losing battle and that all seven of the attorneys were in agreement about this matter. What was really strange is that Timothy never married anyone and there were no other live children to speak of. One of the family heard Albertina say that if she could help it, no one was going to get anything that belonged to Timothy. She set out to do just that out of pure evilness. Her attorney was ruthless, uncouth and it was becoming apparent that he was in it solely to get some of that money. He acted as if it was his business. It was believed by many people in the area that this particular attorney would use any little trick in the book to get what he wanted. Some of the people especially black people in that area who owned land had been tricked into selling their land for little or nothing by this very same attorney. Mama Mary had told the family before all of this started happening that Albertina had turned into some kind of a devious person even though she had always been conniving, but not everybody took heed to what she was saying.

Shortly after the depositions took place the girls were back at the hospital with Mama Mary. They were reflecting about the money episode with Mary and it made them think that maybe she would be alright and the girls decided they were hungry. They went to a Chinese restaurant with their cousin. When they returned, the Dr. was there and almost in tears. She told the girls that Mama Mary had taken a turn for the worse. Her increasingly failing health began quickly. Mama Mary's children all felt a rush of weakness go through their own bodies especially when they had already made plans for a nurse to come to the house and take care of her. Rebecca had a very difficult time accepting what was happening especially since just about the same thing had happened with their father and it didn't help much with her alcohol abuse. This news was not exactly expected because the doctor had previously said that you never know, a miracle might happen and she could pull through this illness. So, again the girls including their cousin Katherine had faith that Mama Mary was going to make it through this episode in her life. It was beginning to look like it was not in God's plan for that to happen. So Elizabeth and Bobbie braced themselves for the worse. They called everybody that they thought needed to be there. They called Aunt Ellen, Uncle Adam, Uncle Paul, Uncle Aaron, and Uncle Frank and told them to please hurry and get to the hospital because they were losing Mama Mary fast. Aunt Ellen brought a beautiful praying cloth and anointing oil to pray for Mama Mary. The cloth was white, blue, gold with gold Hebrew inscriptions that none of them could read. Mama Mary was now on life support just for the rest of the family to get to the hospital and visit with her for the last time. Her breathing began to get softer and softer and softer almost like a new born baby. Her eyes were fixated upwards to one spot in the room and each breath looked as though she was going somewhere beautiful. She looked like a child looking at a toy on the shelf, a toy that she really wanted and had been waiting for a very long time to get it. She looked as though she was not worried about the money, the light bill or the car insurance anymore. She was not worried about her children, whether they were alright or not. All of those worries were lifted from her face.

Her children didn't really accept the loss of their mother at first but somehow reality set in and everybody left the room. As they walked around the hospital they learned that one of their friends had been admitted to the hospital. He had fallen from a ladder and hurt his head pretty bad. Anyone could see that his wife was very distraught about this incident. Apparently, the doctors had told them something that wasn't good because the mortician was there also. Mama Mary's sisters and brothers had to get back on the road to Chicago. They said their goodbyes and left the hospital.

Everybody was in the hallway talking to each other about the good old times and then they decided to walk back over to Mama Mary's room to visit. They kind of knew what to expect because they heard the nurse say that the "fluid in her I.V. was about finished." All of the fluid was now in her body. There was a big difference in her size from when she first went into the hospital. They asked everyone to leave the room so that they could wash her body and change her bedding just as they had done throughout the whole time she was there. Nobody even imagined that anything different was about to happen in a few seconds. It did seem strange since the nurses had been changing her bedding the whole time of her stay with them in the room. The girls were expecting to go back to the room and at least listen to her breathe once again. The nurses came out and said that as they were changing Mama Mary and turned her to the side, she left them all. Everyone tried to remain calm. Mama Mary's club members and friends could not take it. One of the members was crying and said, "I have got to go, I can't stand it." All of her girls were crying, one right after the other. Their brother was home at the time and he knew deep down inside what had happened as the girls tried to console him.

Mama Mary's daughters called the funeral home in Mary's hometown which was in Tennessee. Her body was taken to the airport and then flown to her hometown. Her casket was chosen by two of her daughters, Elizabeth and Bobbie. It was an ivory and pink sprinkled with bronze and bronze handles. The girls decided to wear ivory suits. Mary's son wore a black suit and he was proud of his suit because he hardly ever wore a suit. Mama Mary was dressed in a beautiful dress with pink and white small sparkles all through it. She seemed to be smiling as if she was at peace with herself and with God. Her brothers did the eulogy and sang songs in the church where they said she went to the "moaning bench" each Sunday back around 1943. Her brothers could remember when she became a member of that particular church and they remembered when she went to the pool for baptism. All of her family was there, even her mother who was about twenty years older than her daughter. Mama Mary was laid to rest as close as possible to Papa David whom she never forgot and always wanted to be with. It was a coincidence how both of their mothers lived longer than they did and how both of their fathers passed on before both of their mothers. Some of the relatives prepared an elaborate dinner for the family after the funeral and they were able to sit and talk about happy times with more of the family.

Thank goodness Mama Mary had some money left from her social security disability check which helped with buying her clothes and paying a few bills. She had taken a loan out on her house and the girls didn't know if that would be covered by insurance taking into consideration, her health. Her children were now concerned about paying for this loan or get the house taken away. There was a little bit of bickering over what to do with her material possessions. They felt kind of helpless without her being there with them. Then they began to bicker over the anointing oil and holy scarf of all things that Aunt Ellen left at the hospital. It was finally confirmed after Aunt Ellen spoke with them, that their brother Geoffrey should get those items since he was with Mama Mary most of the time. They were told not to worry about that stuff just stay together as a family and remember the love that they had for their mother.

After the funeral was over, Mary's children were lost without her being around and calling them each and every day. She told them several months before that they were going to miss her calling and bugging them every day. It would be weeks before they patched things up between themselves because some awful, awful hurting things had been said to each other. They still had the chore of cleaning out the house because none of the children wanted to live in the house even though it was built by their father. The house had many good memories in it because they had grown up there and had lots of fun especially at Christmas time when Mama Mary would hide their presents in her closets. When the girls were cleaning the house they couldn't help but to cry after thinking about all of the things that had occurred right there in that house.

Meanwhile, after months and months of depositions and talk about DNA, Albertina's attorney who was now the alleged son's attorney petitioned a motion for DNA testing. The Chancellor decreed that a DNA must be done. Names were given as to who would be willing to give specimens. Uncle John and Uncle Samuel were chosen. At first, one of Timothy's nieces wanted to participate but the diagnostics center only needed the two brothers to complete the test. Albertina's daughter didn't want to have the DNA done because she felt there would possibly be some DNA tampering which had happened before in another case that she knew about. A policeman said, "Oh yes, they do tamper with DNA specimens, they do it all of the time to get what they want." They could even tamper with the reports if they wanted to. She said, "Why should we trust the attorneys when they have already used trickery after we signed the contract?" The defendants didn't want to listen to Albertina's daughter because she was a plaintiff and wanted the alleged son to be a part of the family. One thing Albertina's daughter, she would do any and everything her mother asked her to do. Cousin Katherine said, "We have already been tricked out of a lot, even our grandmother's house is gone all because of one person's greed. Oops! That slipped, I said such a mean thing, but the truth is the light, don't tell me you can't see that that is why we are in this kind of a predicament."

Albertina's daughter said, "But still we thought we had straightened all of that out about this alleged son of Timothy." "Well, now we see that these attorneys can and will use anything you say for or against you," said Katherine.

After Uncle John was notified about DNA, he said, "Well we are going to have to pray really hard and that is all we can do now." Everybody wanted to try and blame someone else for being obligated to have DNA testing. The decree was worded so that no one could blame anyone. Everybody was extremely tired of the case now and didn't want to argue anymore about who really started the mess in the family. All they had to do now was to wait for the lab to send the date and place to take their specimens. They waited for several months, even after the judge had approved the testing and still they had not heard a word. Everybody began to wonder what happened.

They called their attorneys and still they didn't get any real answers except to wait and wait some more. Everybody was so frustrated that they thought of getting different attorneys but it would be very costly and even more time consuming. They knew that the scriptures said, "But they that wait upon the Lord shall renew their strength, they shall mount up with wings as eagles, they shall run and not be weary and thy shall walk and not faint," but after waiting and fighting for ten years and not really getting what they wanted out of the lawsuit, their patience had grown very thin and all they heard the attorneys say was "wait."

It got to the point where everybody said "forget it, let's just get on with our lives because this is too stressful" and some of them had become ill and had given up on life. They began to reflect back on the little school house and how long Mama Julia waited and waited and waited. They began to think about how little they were paid for their inheritance. The inheritance that was kept in the family for nearly a hundred years and their father and grandfather did not want them to ever sell it. They began to think about the years of history. John and Samuel, Jr. tried to comfort them by saying, "Let's not worry about this anymore and be thankful that we still have our families, our sanity and we are blessed to still be able to love one another. You see God has the answers to all of our problems, no matter what people say to you, no matter what kind of mind games people play on you and no matter how people treat you. God is the beginning and the end. A family that prays together stays together. At least the schoolhouse is still standing tall."

While the Strong family was waiting on the finalization of the lawsuit, another startling event took place. Every channel on television was showing the incident. People were running around asking, "Have you heard that a plane flew into the World Trade Center in New York?" Everyone was in a state of shock when that happened. There were two planes that hit the twin towers in New York, the tallest buildings in the world. Not only did they hit the towers, they also hit the Pentagon in Washington, D.C. It was said by many that the terrorist really planned to hit the Capitol building. This was a travesty for the United States and many lives were lost. The president talked about war with Afghanistan and it was announced that the name of the leader of the terrorist plot was known. Elizabeth remembered what Mama Mary said in the year 2000 before she died. Mama Mary said, "Something terrible is going to happen now, I can feel it in my bones." Elizabeth looked around and wondered what in the world could happen. Elizabeth knew that her mother was not feeling well, so she kind of ignored her comment, but not more than three months later the terrorist struck. Mama Mary was already deceased but if only she could have seen what happened, she probably would have been shocked at herself for saying something like that. It wasn't unusual for Mama Mary to predict things that were going to happen. As a matter of a fact, Mama Mary's children were used to her predicting things. It became a normal thing in their household. The Strong family had witnessed something else tragic as they were going through their own family war. Again, they began to think about how blessed they were to still have a family that could still love and care for each other.

The actual war began in the year 2003. It was the conversation of all the citizens in the United States. Mama Josephine became ill and was hospitalized. She had been hospitalized many times since Mama Mary passed away but she tried very hard to stay healthy. The fluid buildup would prevent her from talking like she usually did. Her grandchildren could tell that she just wasn't feeling her old perky self. Mama Josephine didn't want the nurses to check on her, she would tell them to get to work. The nurses wanted to draw blood but Mama Josephine wouldn't let them poke her arm. She was being difficult. Her nieces came in to visit her and told her to be nice and let the nurses draw blood so they can help her. Bobbie went in to see her one day and said, "Hey there pretty lady. How are you doing today?" Mama Josephine perked up real quick then and said, "Doing fine." Mama Josephine loved to be called pretty lady and she always answered when anyone called her that. The nurses learned to do that and Mama Josephine was much easier to get along with after that. The family went to church and had a good old time then they had a birthday party for Mama Josephine and they were waiting for the next birthday party.

Train station similar to where most of the
families boarded for a day of shopping

Born in Memphis, TN in the rural area of Shelby County (Fisherville). Her family moved to the north where she received her education including college diploma at Ball State University. She studied Business Education and Economics. Her interest in Business began in Junior High School and on into High School. Studied English Literature at Ball State University where she met an English Professor with a beautiful accent. It was while she was in college that she had thoughts and dreams of writing a book. She always thought in the back of her mind that her dreams would never happen. Even her dreams of marriage and having a child seemed as though it was impossible. Miraculously, like in her dreams, she did meet her God given, wonderful, supportive and loving husband and she was blessed with a beautiful baby. While working she found time to write. One day she was visiting her second cousin who was 95 years old, she saw a picture of her great-grandparents and was inspired at that moment to sit down and begin her story about the family. While at work, she would type a few words a day and a coworker would remind her to write and that he wanted to read it when it was finished.

It is with her sincere hope that someone young or old, male or female will be inspired by something in this story to follow their dreams no matter what life brings. Even when it seems that there is no hope and that all is a lost cause. Her life example lets us know that you can make life better at the end of the day if that is your desire!